WHEN SPIRIT SPEAKS

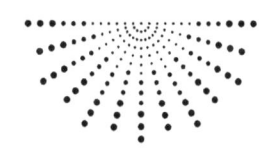

SHARON SALA

When Spirit Speaks

Copyright © 2020 by Sharon Sala

All rights reserved. Except for use in any review, the reproduction or utilization of this work in whole, or in part now known or hereinafter invented, including xerography, photocopying, and recording, or in any information without written permission and consent of the publisher.

This is a work of nonfiction.

Printed in USA

Photo: Depositphotos/@Dink101

Formatting: Pam McCutcheon/Parker Hayden Media

Cover Design: The KILLION Group, Inc.

A NOTE FROM THE AUTHOR

SPIRIT TALKS TO ME.
I didn't ask for this gift.
For years, I didn't even know what it was.
I've always been led by an inner voice that I thought everyone heard.
But the weird thing for me is...I don't hear it with my ears. It's like a thought that suddenly pops into my mind, and I know it's something I'm supposed to share, or it's something I'm supposed to remember to tell someone else when the time is right, and it won't let me go until I write it down and send it out.
All I have to do is put my fingers on a keyboard, and Spirit's message starts coming through, as clear to me as a radio signal.

I'm not psychic.
I don't even pretend to be.
The closest thing I can come to explaining me is that, I am a messenger.
And so, in that respect, when Spirit talks, I just deliver the messages.
They've never been singular messages to just one person.

They're always messages that address humanity.

I've been posting them on a social media site for years - because it is the only way I know how to deliver the messages to the broadest audience.

Sometimes Spirit's messages will be for certain portion of the population suffering a specific thing, whether it's health or personal issues.

And sometimes, Spirit's messages are for everyone.

They aren't always easy to hear.

There are many times I don't want to pass them on, because I know I'm going to get flack about it, because the messages often read like being scolded by a parent who loves you dearly.

But I've long since given up receiving the complaints personally.

All it is, is someone recognizing themselves in the messages, and reacting to what they've done to themselves, or where the path they're on is leading them.

Some days, I feel like I'm just "preaching to the choir", so to speak.

That the only people who care what I post, are already on their own paths of a righteous life.

But it's not for me to judge who receives, or complain about what Spirit sends.

The love in the Spirit-led words, comes from God.

I am but a facilitator to get them to you.

The messages in this book are a compilation of posts from my social media sites, but the messages are clear and timeless, and they do not have expiration dates.

What was God-given, is always good to know.

Read what I am sharing.

Receive what you need, and go with God.

Sent with peace.

Sent with light.

Sent with love.

WHEN SPIRIT SPEAKS

I once heard a whippoorwill call from a nearby field, but it got no answer.

The little bird then moved from field to fence, from fence to tree, calling, calling without a response. And then far off I heard another call - the same mournful cry - and at that moment, the little whippoorwill took flight.

It was no longer lost.

It was no longer alone.

Spirit says:

Being alone.

Feeling alone in a crowd of people is a common feeling to all of us at one time or another.

Like the little whippoorwill, we yearn to belong.

Yet for some people, the courage it takes to enter a conversation is often impossible.

So think about this...how does one communicate if this is how they move through life?

Being fearful...waiting for someone else to make the first move, being afraid to speak up - to ask for help - to simply say your name and hold out your hand as you meet someone new...is living a fear-based life.

You cannot do what you came here to do if you're afraid to smile at a stranger.

Do you speak to strangers when you're standing in line?

Can you find common ground by simply smiling and saying hello?

This is the way of the world, and yet you are reticent to accept it.

Staying in an insular world, being only with the people you know and grew up with, is a choice, but it can become a sad, solitary existence.

The next time you soul cries out for company....seek those among you with the brightest lights.

Sent with peace.
Sent with light.
Sent with love.

I AM THE MESSENGER.

I am a total stranger to millions...and I am still praying for you.
Loving and honoring your existence.
You think you are alone?
You think you don't matter, that no one cares about you?
Well, I care.
God cares.
We are all part of the Great I am.
Part of the whole of the white light in heaven, and you are SO LOVED in the best possible way.
I send you love every day...not just on special occasions.

I pray for you every night without fail.

When you go to bed tonight all alone and you're feeling sad, or lost as to why you are in the place you are in at this moment in your life.... Think of me...praying for you.

When you wake up in the morning, and feel overwhelmed by the adulation others are receiving, Think of me... Loving you.

❧

Spirit says:
Everything is energy.
You. Me. Animals. Inanimate objects.
Trees. Mountains.
Water. Air. Fire. Earth.
Even color and sound. They're all different vibrations of energy.

When you look out a window and see the street, and cars driving on it...or grass, and children playing in the yard...whatever it is...you are really looking at different vibrations of energy.

Think about when you are happy...how elated you suddenly feel inside. How beautiful everything is to you that day. It looks different to you, because you raised your own vibration by being happy, and in doing so, you saw the world as it truly is. Your personal vibration allowed you to see a greater truth.

If the world you see is drab, and sad, and you live in a constant state of anger, fear, or depression, your personal vibration in that place is very low, so what you 'see' through that level of energy is a direct reflection of how you feel. You can't see beauty, unless you first feel it.

This is why living in a state of calm and peace matters.

Why focusing on love and kindness matters.

Those emotions are to your spirit, what turning up the heat is to a cold room.

Like turning on a light in the dark.

Becoming the light in the darkness.

You don't know how to feel happy?

Get out of your own head. If all you think about is your lack.

Then poverty in all aspects of your life is where you'll stay, because the energy you have focused on your expectations is too low to grow - to prosper in all aspects of living.

Spirit says:

You are free at all times to laugh, to share, to help, to comfort, to shelter, to become. And each time you find joy in something, or see the beauty in something, reach out in kindness to someone, be the peacemaker, or give love to someone, your energy rises...and rises...and rises...until you have become a different person in everyone's eyes. They won't know why you're different, but they'll see it, and your world will change in ways you cannot, at this moment, imagine.

Why?

Because you are manifesting energy...and when you can bring joy to yourself by the simple acts of daily kindness and love, you will be bringing tangible prosperity as well by simply thinking about it.

Love vibrates at the energy of 528 Hz.

The energy of the Fifth Dimension of the Universe begins at 500.

It's like moving to a higher floor in a high-rise apartment. Earth is still here, but you are seeing it, and living in it, in a higher level of understanding.

You just walked out of a dim room, into another room in the same house that's filled with light.
When you raise your energy...that's what you get.
Same principal. Same result.
What are you waiting for?
Turn on the light within you by tuning into the Universal message.
"Love one another, as I have loved you."

Sent with peace.
   Sent with light.
   Sent with love.

&a;

Sometimes as something wonderful is happening to us, we say..."I never dreamed this could happen".
I'm sure I've said it in the past.
But I know now this isn't the right way to chase a dream.
ALWAYS speak aloud your dreams in a positive mindset.
MY dreams are reality.
Even when they're not quite there yet, just putting that positive message out into the Universe and believing it, ups your energy and makes those "things you never dreamed come true."

So when I was writing the post above, a timer went off in the kitchen for my baked potato. I hit Send, and then go to the kitchen to take it out of the oven.
I opened the door, went to pick up the potato with a pot holder, and the potato BLEW THE HECK UP IN MY HAND.
Talk about shock. TALK ABOUT A MESS. I stand there looking down in disbelief...and what do you think came out of my mouth? "I can't remember the last time this happened."

The very minute I said it, I started laughing. I'd just experienced the very thing I'd written.

"Okay guys! I get the joke!" I said aloud, and the energy that shot through me, made every hair on my body stand on end. Angels were laughing with me. I'm still laughing...and I'm still feeling the ripples of energy.

I know who's laughing most.

My Bobby...who is in spirit.

The man who gave the best hugs.

The man with the booming laugh, and a joy for life that knew no boundaries.

You win, baby. The joke's on me!

୨⚬

When my sister and I were eleven and twelve, my mother, a school teacher who suffered from back trouble most of her life, hurt her back just as the school year was ending, and couldn't move without severe pain. She needed a walker, but those kinds of things weren't available then, so she turned one of the wooden chairs from our dining room set, so that the back of the chair was closest to her, put an old bath mat beneath all four legs so it would slide, and used it like a walker, pushing that chair all over the hardwood floors in our house.

And because she was incapacitated, it fell to my younger sister and I to take care of the house, which meant cleaning, cooking, and laundry, and hoeing and watering the huge garden all by ourselves, that we'd planted earlier in the year. It was a monumental job, but there weren't any options. Mother depended on us, and we all depended on that food to get us through the winter because money was so scarce in our world.

When it came time to start harvesting crops from the garden, we knew what to do, because we'd been canning food for 4-H club projects for a while, and we'd always helped mother can what we grew in the garden every year.

I look back now at what we accomplished that summer, as something of a small miracle. We picked bushels of green beans in the early morning before it got hot, and then spent all day breaking and canning them, filling our pressure cooker with quart jars ready to process and seal. That pressure cooker were so heavy. I don't know how we lifted it, but we did. We canned beets and beet pickles, and potatoes. We froze sweet corn, canned tomatoes, and tomato juice. We froze strawberries, and canned applesauce. We canned vegetable soup, and three kinds of pickles. And never once complained, because we were already scared seeing Mother in such misery.

When Daddy came home from work, he carried all the cooled jars down into the cellar, and brought up a new batch of empty quart jars for us to wash, so we would be ready to do it all over again the next day.

Between the rest Mother got that summer, plus a few trips to a chiropractor, she healed enough to start back to teaching in the fall.

That whole winter, every time Mother opened a jar of green beans, or beet pickles, or got a bag of frozen corn from the freezer, or thawed out a bag of fruit, or opened a quart of vegetable soup, she would hug us. Every time.

It was the first time I realized what being family really meant. It wasn't just living under the same roof, or looking like each other, or having the same last name. It was doing what had to be done for the good of all.

I left my childhood in that garden.

I had a confidence I'd never felt before.

I didn't just get taller that summer.

I grew up.

I learned true empathy for others suffering.

I learned a lesson, and that's what getting through the hard times is all about.

§

It's cold and rainy here today. Not sticking my nose out of the house at all unless I have to. I want to be in the kitchen baking, with a pot of vegetable beef soup bubbling on the stove. But since I can't eat anything with meat anymore without suffering health issues, I'll settle for not blowing up another baked potato in the oven.

Spirit says:

Finding joy in the small things is the goal for today.

A phone call from a granddaughter, sharing a laugh with someone, cherishing the sound of a beloved's voice over the phone -- just being grateful for the warmth and warm clothes.

Most of you who have known me for years, know I grew up in rural Oklahoma, and at a time when electricity had yet to be strung down our red dirt roads, and when running water meant, running outside to the well to draw a bucket of water. So I learned at an early age to be grateful for the small things.

One of those things I remember as being special was getting new underwear. We wore ours until the elastic was gone, and there was nothing left to sew up. Nearly all of little girl panties at the time were cotton, but the day my mother came home with some new underwear for my younger sister, Diane, and me, and it was the silky kind like she wore, we were beside ourselves with joy.

It was such a simple thing. Nothing anyone would ever see. Just a special thing for us. A sweet thing to remember.

Lately, I've been cleaning out drawers, and as I came to my lingerie drawer, I realized how worn out some of my underwear was getting. So yesterday I bought myself some new ones to replace what I was discarding. I ran it all through the laundry after I got home, and this morning as I was dressing, the weirdest thing happened. Just for just a moment, I flashed back to that morning of my childhood, when a new pair of panties was the best thing ever, and then I smiled.

I've come a long way, baby, from a little girl in the country. But at heart, I guess I will always be a country girl, because new underwear still rocks my world.

🙵

As a farmer's daughter, and then a farmer's wife, my life was lived according to the seasons. In Oklahoma, where I was born and raised, Spring was a time of planting, but also the time of storms. I have no idea how many times I planted seeds or young plants, only to have then washed out, or beaten down by the storms. But such was the way of that life, and I would simply replant that which had been destroyed.

Spirit says:

So it is with life. We have hope and purpose, and we are sowing the seeds of our future, and making plans, when we are suddenly pulled into a life storm. Whether it be the chaos of a broken marriage, or grief from the sudden loss of a loved one, or a job loss, or the onset of a debilitating illness, we feel uprooted, like the newly planted seeds. We have no anchor to this reality, and so we bounce about in storms of emotional trauma, until something triggers us, and we manage to pull ourselves upright and go on. It isn't easy to grow new roots, but if the will to fight, is stronger than the urge to quit, we survive.

Spirit says:
We aren't 'given' life. We're already alive before we come here, and living in perfect harmony with God and the Universe.

When we, as souls, agree to come here, it is for purpose.

We come to atone for mistakes made in a previous human life. Or we come to grow our empathy and understanding of what being human is all about. We come to serve. Or to teach. And some come to experience true suffering, knowing the only way to really understand it, is to experience it.

Life on earth is a school.

Life back home is our perfection.

But to be able to live a human life, all our memories of home are taken away for the time that we are here. It is part of the lesson.

Using only the love and kindness we brought with us, we learn to weather the storms of this life, and be strong enough to put down new roots when we are torn by the troubles.

That is why we're here. Not as competitors. Not as enemies. But as tiny sparks of God-light, growing and spreading our own light into the atmosphere of this one tiny planet, tucked away in a corner of the vastness of the Universe that is God.

Spirit says:
Running away from trouble doesn't leave it behind.
Until an issue you've had in life has been resolved, it will ride your conscience, and burden your heart your entire life, until you face it, and deal with it.

It's like a lie. The longer it goes with truth being revealed, the bigger it grows, until there are so many layers of guilt attached to you, that it affects every other aspect of your life.

Praying about it won't make it go away.

God doesn't fix our mistakes, nor solve our troubles. He gives us strength to face it, but He does not interfere with free will. That which you have chosen to say or do, is also yours to apologize for. It's yours to make right.

If it's something you feel you can't face alone, ask for help, but don't leave a wake of wrong-doing tied to your future and your path.

I used to be a people-watcher at the mall. I would find a place to sit and rest between errands, and make up stories about the people who passed by me. (It's the writer in me. We all do it.)

But that was before...and this is now...and I can't do that anymore, because the Shift in Earth's energy has upped the Empath in me, to the point that I can just look at a person and cry.

I feel their despair. I feel their fears. The worst ones are the ones filled with so much rage that it's choking and frightening.

Sometimes it's a feeling that comes so unexpected that I have no time to refocus, and I'm sitting in my car at a stoplight sobbing because of the young homeless man who just walked in front of my car, like what happened today.

He was tall and thin...so thin. His coat wasn't heavy enough for the cold, and he was clutching a bottle of Mountain Dew with both hands, holding it against his chest. His gait was halted, and the lost expression on his face undid me.

The despair I felt from him was crippling, and when the light turned green, all I could do was say a prayer for him, and then tell myself all the way the way home it was his path to walk, not mine, not mine.

As you can tell, I haven't been able to let that one go yet, but I will. In time, someone else will wipe me out, and once again, I'll be struggling to get past what I feel.

Every night I pray for a world where homelessness does not exist, and where people with mental illnesses are not turned out onto the streets because they're too much trouble to deal with.

In the world I imagine, kindness and love are the bywords, and peace exists.

Earth as it exists right now is poison to me. I pray every day for something better - where people are kind, and making fun of others is not a venue for entertainment. I'm not made that way, and being around people who are, hurts my heart.

Be the Light, people. Be the Love.

Find a way to be a kinder, gentler you.

※

I made potato salad this morning to have a quick side dish already prepared for upcoming meals. I like potato salad when I first make it best, before it's had time to get cold.

I'm waiting "again" on a plumber to come light the pilot in my gas fireplace this afternoon. The one that was supposed to come yesterday evening never showed. It is times like these that I sure miss my Bobby. He could do anything.

Today when I was walking down the short hall from my bedroom to the kitchen, I flashed on the long hallway between my childhood bedroom and the long hallway between it and the living room/kitchen, and wished in that moment that, when I reached the end of my hallway now, I would walk into my kitchen and Mother would be making breakfast, and Daddy would be leaving for work, or still asleep from working swing shift.

It was just a moment - and then the thought was gone. But wanting to hide from our present realities is a normal emotion - an understandable feeling when there are things off kilter in our lives that we can't control. When we aren't supposed to try and fix it, and we have to let happen what will happen.

There are many ways for a heart to break, and many ways to deal with the aftermath. None of them are easy, and finding a way to live with what is, and let go of what was, or what you wanted, is the lesson to be learned.

If you can't find comfort for your soul, comfort your body instead. Play your favorite music, wear your favorite 'at home' clothing. Wrap yourself in something soft and warm, and settle into the most comfortable chair or sofa you own, then close your eyes.

Let go of world problems. Work problems. Family problems. Relationship problems.

Give them to God and let go.

Heal yourself.
Love yourself.
Be at peace.

Spirit Says:
We have become a nation of excess in material things, and yet there is a scarcity in many of us, for caring what happens to others.

Some hold beauty, money, and power, as the guidelines to success, and walk on the back of the less fortunate to get it.

You can justify your actions to yourself, and to others, but in God's eyes, you cannot talk your way out of what you've said and done to get your way.

Understand that this life you're living now impacts everyone around you. Even when you say it's your life to live.

It's the same thing as being a little kid and going to play in the mud, even when you know you shouldn't. All those around you will be muddy, too. Every step you take will leave muddy tracks of where you've been. When you take it into your home, you will be leaving mud all over your house, and on your family.

You can wash it off your body, and you can wash it off your clothes, but there will be places where the stains won't wash off.

So it is with the lives we live. When we hurt the ones who love us, we also hurt ourselves.

Be thoughtful of your words.

Be thoughtful of how you walk in the world.

Be the light for others.

Be at peace.

Be kind.

Be Love.

༺ ༻

Spirit Says:

We are known to others in many ways. By our name...by the familiarity of our face...by our occupation...by a deed...by a mistake...by a grievous sin.

But that's still not who we are. That is something we were either born with, or what we did.

You do not let someone else define who you are.

You have purpose here...and whatever you'd done to give credence to your existence so far, may have nothing to do with why you're here.

Be true to yourself.

Even if you have chosen a selfish path...it still does not define who you are...only what you've done.

Someone else's opinion of you is theirs, not yours.

We aren't meant to sacrifice ourselves, to make life easier for someone else. But at the same time, we also do not shirk the responsibilities we have accrued.

If through your free will, you have borne children, then they must become part of your path...not something to leave behind when you suddenly have an urge to chase a dream.

You can't run fast enough, or far enough, to escape that mistake.

And you don't need to be on your own, to do what you came here to do.

Sometimes it's the family around you that lifts you up and gives you the strength you need to believe in yourself.

There's a fine line in life between who we are, and the roles we play, and it's up to us to find the balance.

Believe.
Be the Light.
Be the Love.

Spirit says:

Challenges are a part of life.

Every day we are faced with at least one new challenge, sometimes more. Sometimes they're connected, and then there are the days when it's one after the other, and the world is falling in on you, and you alone. You can't see past the frustration or the devastation. You can't think past trying to figure out which one to deal with first, or if it would be simpler to just go to bed, and hope it's all over in the morning.

. . .

I've been on the receiving end of these moments.

We all have.

The trick is how to go about working through it. Which one do you deal with first, and what is it going to take to make that happen?

What you have to remember is you aren't the only one with troubles, and that this too shall pass.

I've told you in other books, at other times, that Bobby was my childhood sweetheart, and then we lost touch. Forty years later, he reappeared in my life when I was going through a bitter divorce. His presence led me out of a very dark place. He was always the love of my life, and now he'd come back into my life - like the angel I needed him to be. He was a recovering alcoholic. His life had been troubled, and a lot of it was hard and sad.

The thing about him that no amount of liquor could ever change, was his love for humanity, and his 'don't quit' mindset.

When we finally found each other again, after all those years apart, he was celebrating several years of sobriety.

And since I grew up the child of an alcoholic, I had great respect for him. My Daddy tried to quit drinking for years, but it took his own fear of dying to make him quit.

As for Bobby, he had his own ways of coping.

The one thing I remember most was that open bottle of whiskey he kept on the top shelf of his closet. The first time I saw the half-empty bottle, he told me it was the last bottle of whiskey he'd bought, and that after he got sober, he took it with him, everywhere he'd moved.

It wasn't a test to see if he could look at it without wanting a drink. As he said many times, "There's never a day when I don't want one."

The whiskey was there to remind him that he had suffered far worse things, than whatever was happening on that day.

It was the reminder for him of what he'd already conquered.
But that was just his proof.
It was God that gave him the strength.
I had eight of the most blessed years of my life before he died - in my arms. Cancer ended his time here.
God took him home.

Whatever it is you think of when you're trying to figure a way out of your problems, just remember it isn't your first rodeo. You've had trouble before and lived through it. You will do it again.
So take a breath.
Go to that place within you where your secrets are kept.
Say a prayer, but don't ask God to fix it.
Ask God for the wisdom to find the answers, and the strength to see it through.

Sent with peace.
Sent with light.
Sent with love.

I pray Peace for you.
I pray Love.
I pray for silence when discord begins.

Spirit says:
When you are shouting to be heard, your voice becomes lost in the cacophony around you.
If you cannot be heard, then step out of the crowd, and walk away.
Reason does not exist where there is anger and rage.

Other than wanting to cause a disturbance, why state your opinion when it was not asked for?

If you don't like where you are, and what is being said, your best move it to get up and leave, rather than start arguing, and trading verbal and physical blows.

At that point, no one cares what you think, because you have exhibited your willingness to hurt others just to be right.

Sent with peace.
    Sent with light.
    Sent with love.

I am reflecting on this cold Sunday morning, thinking of how many times I have awakened to a day like this, and with similar thoughts as I have now.

I think of myself as the sum of three parts - the lives I have lived - the life I am living now - and the soul I am.

My soul is constant and it is my eternal connection to the Great I Am. It has taken me most of this lifetime to come to the understanding of how connected we are to the Source.

Spirit says:

An earthly light can be extinguished, but heavenly light goes on forever, and we are ALL part of the heavenly light.

If you are living a fear-based life, know that you're never alone.

Even if you've forgotten where you came from, God has not forgotten you.

Even if you don't believe, or are not aware, your guardian angels are always at your side. They aren't allowed to interfere in your free will...but they are your unseen support system.

. . .

I talk to my angels, just like I talk to Bobby in spirit. I don't ask them to solve my problems, but I have often asked them to 'show me' the way. To open my eyes...so that I might find what I've lost...so that I might make my own choices, and to find my path again.

I am living a life alone. But I don't ever feel alone.

I didn't say I don't get lonely. I said, I don't ever feel alone in my space.

I am ever-aware of the unseen world around me.

And I take comfort in knowing the thread of God-light that links me to home is never broken.

Take comfort in knowing you have come this way before - that what's happening to you now is, in the time of God, but a blink of an eye.

Remember always, 'this, too, shall pass."

Sent with peace.
    Sent with light.
    Sent with love.

Remember that picture I posted a couple of days ago of all those books in my floor?

Well, they're gone now. I couldn't look at Mother's books all stacked up in the floor another day. She's gone. It took her nearly 99 years to leave this earth, and the last years of her life, she didn't remember who she was, and she didn't know me. Fourteen years of being lost in dementia is finally over for her, and I thank God.

But I had to find a place to donate all those books...so the Friends of the Library was my outlet.

Only now my back hurts. My left ankle is swollen now from making so many trips to the car, and I'm exhausted.

But they're gone, and I don't have to talk about them, or look at them anymore.

Giving away pieces of someone else's life hurts my heart.

It was just as hard to give away my mother's clothes, as it was her books, but such is life, and it does go on.

I have things to do, and purpose, as yet, incomplete.

Spirit says:

Let go of your anger at people who do not see life the way you do. It is not possible for them to see through your eyes, or with your understanding, in the same way it is not possible for you to understand why they are how they are.

We aren't clones. We aren't meant to gather in like-minded herds. We don't have the right to interfere with other people's lives.

We are sovereign souls on our own separate journeys, so when you meddle into someone else's business, that means you have abandoned your purpose, just to interfere with someone else.

Be the best YOU can be. Shovel your own dirt, lay your own bricks, and don't worry about the life someone else is building.

It will never be yours to inhabit.

I'm getting a massage this morning.
Writing by the fire this afternoon.
The day is a good one because I deem it so.
I am open and receptive to all good.
I am safe. I am always protected. I am enough.
I do not acknowledge the dark side.
It does not exist in my world.
If you prepare for the worst, it will come, because you invited it when you began to prepare.

It's like cooking dinner for a family gathering.

You expect them because you invited them, and so you are preparing for their arrival.

The same holds true for what some people call bad luck, or tough breaks.

That which you expect you will get, because the Universe answers.

It does not distinguish between fear and desire...only the energy of the emotion you put out.

Look for the light in all things great and small.

Don't wait for someone else to make you happy.

Create your own joy.

You have the power.

Use it.

Spirit Says:
Following your passion is guided by inner persistence.
You HAVE to believe in yourself first.

It's a given.

Even if you've been turned down at the next step to your dream, time and time again, that means nothing except that, you either weren't in the right place, or it wasn't the right time.

When you know what you know - that you were born to do something specific - that everything in your life has led you right to the doorstep of what you want to do - then push through.

Don't take NO for an answer.

Keep looking for another way to get where you want to go.

There are many paths, and many doors in life, but eventually they all lead to where you're meant to be.

If you believe.

Sent with peace.
    Sent with light.
    Sent with love.

Spirit says:

If you are nursing a wound that someone else caused, and waiting for an apology before you move on...that's the same thing as suffering an open wound, then waiting for the person who hurt you to stop the bleeding.

You wouldn't lie there and choose to bleed to death, so why choose to suffer hurt feelings for so long that they turn into anger within you?

Like the infection you would get if you did not seek help for a physical injury?

The words that hurt you then, are still hurting you now because you're holding them in your heart.

You don't need anyone else's permission to cast them out.

Just say aloud...."You have no power over me. Your words are little more than dust in my eyes that I have long since washed out. You gave me your anger...I send back my love."

Then let it be, and you are free.

Sent with peace.
    Sent with light.
    Sent with love.

Spirit says:

When you have lost your way, life can seem like a scavenger hunt.

Someone tells you about a product that will make you pretty, and you're off to find it. Or you are looking for a lifestyle to make you slim. Or looking for a job that will make you rich. Or looking for a man to take care of you.

What you seek can't be put on your face, or put into your body.

Money isn't going to fill you up, and you don't need someone else to take care of you, when all that you need is already within you.

Stop asking everyone else for their opinions about what you should do, and make a decision for yourself. It is an empowering feeling to do that. It's your life. You make the choices that impact it, and if the choices you made were wrong, then make some different ones.

You make trivial, frivolous decisions without blinking an eye, and then waver when it comes to things that matter.

Trust yourself.
Love yourself.
Be you.

※

If I was still out on the farm, the garden would have been turned over, and I would be running the tiller to get the ground worked, and ready for planting.

I would have my stakes, and the line I used to make straight rows, and all of my seed packets would be in a box waiting for me to put them in the ground.

We'd have the Farmer's Almanac out looking for the right sign to plant the potatoes under, and Daylight Savings would be two words that meant nothing to me.

I was getting ready to create...to plant, to tend, to hoe and water, to grow the food we'd eat.

Do I miss it?
Not the work.
Do I miss the country?
With every breath that I take.
I wasn't born to be a city girl.
There isn't anything about it that I like except the convenience of going to the grocery store.

I am a simple person. It doesn't take much to please me, and nearly all of it revolves around my family.

Or at least it did.

Part of my family does not communicate with me anymore, and part of them have gone their own way. I wish them well. I send love and healing to all of them every day. But such is life.

One day I won't even be here anymore, and they'll still have to get up and face each day just as I'm doing now. Accepting that life changes and people change with it.

It's how things are supposed to be.

I am still creating. Today, I will write another chapter in the book in progress.

I won't talk to a soul unless I leave the house or someone calls. Or if I decide to talk to Bobby, which I do quite often.

I can't hear him, but he can hear me, and that's enough.

Sometimes I miss his physical presence to the point of pain, but again...that's life.

And life never ends...it just changes form.
We are energy before we come here.
We are energy in another form while we are human.

And we are energy again when we go home...but hopefully...if we've done things right here...if we're on the path and teaching or learning what we came here to do... we are a brighter, whiter light when we return.

So today I honor the soul I am...the hundreds of lives I've lived before...the life I'm living now, along with all the good and bad that came with it...and every day, I create the world in which I want to live, both on paper, and in real time...by action and by words.

I choose to be happy, even when it's hard.
I choose to let go of things that are not mine to hold.
I choose Light.
I choose Peace.
I choose Love.

When I was a little girl, I had no aspirations beyond the small world in which I existed.

As I grew a little older, my world expanded to the possibilities of what came with being an adult.

When I became that adult, I thought my world was complete. Over. Finished. That there would be nothing more than existing and raising my children, then watching my grandchildren grow up, and growing old among this huge, loving family.

I had not taken into consideration the losses that would come, or the changes in my life that would come with them.

I never imagined becoming a writer.

Ever.

I didn't think the stories in my head were anything more than how my brain worked...just random thoughts that helped me pass the time as I worked on the farm.

I didn't know that everything that had happened to me from

my earliest memory to the age of 47, when I wrote my first book, was preparing me for the shift that was about to happen in my life.

I didn't know my daydreams were going to turn into stories, that would turn into books, that would eventually be read around the world.

I didn't know.

But what I did learn as that new part of my life began, was that every kind and gentle thing I had witnessed in my life, began to spill into my stories. Every hero I had as a child, became that larger than life hero I put in my books. Every heroine I wrote about came from the prototypes of the real heroines I'd known.

And I knew without ever being told, that every story had to come full circle before it had ended, because that's how I saw life.

I find the good in my characters...even the bad ones...and often leave it to the reader to judge them, because I cannot find it in me to judge.

Even the people who have hurt me most.

There is a part of me who still believes the hurt they caused is part of my path - that they were part of the lessons I needed to learn, and that when I go home one day, we'll meet in spirit again and rejoice, thanking each other for the help they gave, so that I might learn the lessons I'd come here to learn.

I tell you this now, so that you might see life through a new window. That you might be able to find it in your heart to forgive your enemies...to move past old wounds and look only to the future...to a new path...a new way of living.

In this hard and broken time in our history, it is imperative that you let go of hate and vengeance, because those emotions will not serve you. They will be the hindrance in your life that keeps you from moving forward.

We have to let go of the old ways.

The ways that we were slaves to: The mindset of constant debts and taxes as being normal. The mindset of accepting that, some people have food, and shelter, and access to health care, and others don't. The mindset of being told what to think and how to live. And ridding yourself of the mindset that people with power and money are right.

There is a change in humanity waiting for all of us, but you have to choose.

Will you choose the old way of wars, and enemies, and prejudice, and rage?

Or will you choose the way of light, love, and peace?

You can no longer be on the fence about your beliefs and raise your energy.

You cannot grow the light within you if your heart is cold to human suffering.

It's so simple.

Pray Light for all.
    Pray Peace for all.
    Pray Love for all.
    And mean it.

※

I went back to Prague, OK today for my Aunt Neta Smith's funeral. She was born Marjorie Oneta Musgrove, and married Glenn Smith, one of my daddy's younger brothers. They both graduated from Paden High School...the same school I graduated from, as well.

She was 96. Another sweet family member gone. My love and prayers were with her daughter, Sheri Porterfield, and her family.

It was a beautiful day. My cousins and I talked about it when we went out to the cemetery. I don't know why, but sunshine and blue skies dotted with perfect white clouds, makes leaving a loved one at a cemetery just a little bit easier. As we were leaving, I saw a large flock of birds take flight from a nearby tree, and circle the area before flying away.

They said during the service that Aunt Neta loved birds...feeding the birds, watching the birds... I think they came to honor a kindred spirit. But that's just me and my native heart reading nature into life, and life into nature.

What you give out in life is given back to you tenfold, and today Aunt Neta's loving heart was honored that way.

I wore my Navajo jewelry to the service. Sleeping Beauty turquoise...Navajo silver. I felt the need to be grounded and protected with that today. I don't know exactly why, but I always honor the instincts that move me.

I honor the Old Ones. My Cherokee and Cree ancestors. I honor my elders. I always heed their words.

At this age, there aren't many of them left, which makes them that much more precious to me.

Soon, my generation in that family will be the eldest.

Nothing to be sad about. It's just life, and so it goes.

Be at peace today.
It matters.

LOOK BEYOND THE OBVIOUS

In a country where scandal is the soup du jour, and outrage is the sought-after emotion of the dark side - know that you are being played. Pay attention to how it's doled out to the masses, just as a crisis has been dealt with or averted, another so-called scandal 'rocks' the news.

So far, none of it is new, and none of it is news.

We don't need to know the names of madmen and murderers. Mention it only when they're arrested, and let their notoriety die like the people they killed.

Honor the victims.

The current scandal is the rich people buying their kids way into college...and from the way it is being reported it's just two rich women...although we know over 40 people...mostly the faces of men, are safely hidden in the shadows of these two who have been sacrificed as the two people to hate.

And you know how much we love to hate. And how happy our hate makes the dark side feel, because it feeds the negativity that keeps all of this ugly world in motion.

If only you would stop buying into this mindset....

Spirit sends this message over and over again.

I say it over and over again to you, but believing all of the negativity is so addictive to you now that you don't want to hear truth. You just want to be right.

Someone needs to speak up, you say, and speaking becomes shouting, becomes rage, becomes retribution...and here we are...still stuck in a medieval mindset.

Where the hell is the hot tar? We don't need a wall. We already have a moat. It's called the Rio Grande.

. . .

But the truth is much simpler...and we never cared before...because the dark side didn't need that trigger to set us off, until it mattered for them, and the retention of their power.

Rich people have been buying their kids way into institutions of higher learning for centuries. That's nothing new. But for now...it has become this huge scandal suddenly uncovered.

Only it was never a secret. Not by a long shot.

For centuries they have 'endowed'. They 'sponsored'. They 'donated', and their names were carved in stone on the new wings of some building, and their kids were ensured a place in the elite places of higher learning.

So while all that stuff is taking place, look at what's NOT being covered in the news.

Most of the state of Nebraska has, and still is suffering horrendous flooding. Not a word from government...not FEMA - not the Red Cross, nothing.

There are still communities along the gulf shore in Alabama that were impacted by the hurricane that swept through there LAST YEAR and NOTHING has been offered to them in the way of help. We ignored the entire existence of Puerto Rico after a hurricane, and still do, and it is a U.S. Territory.

And what are we all focused on right now? Oh yes! A wall.

What are being led to? A repeat of East and West Berlin? Trying to build an updated version of The Great Wall of China?

I roll my eyes at the blind mania this mass hysteria incurs.

Why are we still, after thousands and thousands of years of war that solved nothing....still fighting? WHY?

Do you know how many times civilization has destroyed itself because of this very behavior?

How many innocent people died during thousands of years of fighting for what a few powerful people wanted?

That's what war is all about. That's what a wall means. Keeping out people you feel threatened by. Proclaiming there is no crime among us, and that the threat to our safety comes from them, when it is people born in this country who are the mass murderers. They're the killers. They're the human traffickers. They're the drug dealers. And THEY are controlled by the faceless billionaires who control us all. Our mindset is slavery.

We are slaves to their whims. Puppets to the strings they pull.

A thousand of them will commit crimes against humanity, and at the bidding of the people who own the media, we become focused not on the real dangers - but on poor people - women and children fleeing from wars, and migrant workers just wanting a better life for their families, which are the very reasons white people ever came to this land - seeking religious freedom. Seeking a better life. And what did they do to get it?

They stole this land. They killed to get it. And then they called it theirs. And thus the darkness began all over again.

The legacy of the dark side will reflect in the ages to come...that their presence in this place called the United States of America, was the beginning of the end. Again.

Spirit says:
LOOK BEYOND THE OBVIOUS.

さ

Spirit says:
Being true to yourself shows in how you speak, and how you act toward others.

Sometimes your truth, spoken aloud, will hurt others.

So think about it a moment.

If what you believe and practice will hurt others because they don't believe as you do, then how can that be resolved?

If you don't care that you go through life hurting other people, then that's your choice. That's the free will you came with.

I can't say that your soul's reception will be quite the homecoming you expect when this life is done, if you have not followed the one rule you came with. "Do unto others, as you would have them do unto you."

So, what's your solution?

Maybe think before you speak?

Live and think the way you please, but don't harm others in the process?

Maybe you could slip that "Judge not, lest ye also be judged," into your daily life?

Or not.

It's all about that free will. Just know that calling yourself a good person, and then belittling and judging, harming both by word and deed, makes you a liar.

If you truly believe you are better than other people just because of how you worship, and how you dress, and where you live, then so it is.

Just remember that you bring to you, that of which you speak.

The messages are clear.

The world is changing for the better.

If you deny the need - or fight the changes of love, peace, and kindness to ALL, then you are going to become the ones who are singled out, and ignored.

As always, the choices are yours.

Pick one and be true to the person you need to be.

※

It has stayed cloudy and overcast all day. I even had the gas fireplace on for a little while.

I ran a couple of errands after lunch and was fortunate to run into an old friend in the west-side Walmart. She didn't recognize me because the last time we saw each other, I probably weighed about 250 lbs, or more. That was before Weight Watchers, and so long ago I guess I'd forgotten. When she finally mentioned she didn't recognize me at first because of the weight loss, it was kind of a neat thing to hear, so that was my good thing today.

A weird thing - but not necessarily weird for me - I left the house with my phone charged at 85%. Did not use it once while I was out, and when I got home, I got a little 'low battery' notice and looked down. It was at 25% and falling. So I put it on the charger. Spirits do that when they're around. But again, this is part of my life, so what else is new?

I had a dream the other night that I was buried beneath the earth. I was on my side and even though it was dark, I could still see the dark loam and the little bits of stuff within it. I just laid there staring at the dirt and wondering why I was there.

Two days later, it hit me.

It's about rebirth.

Moving into a higher consciousness.

That's what happens to you when you live a life of conscious purpose, believing everyone is entitled to be loved, healed, sheltered, and fed...that we all have purpose that we follow, whether it's learning lessons or teaching them.

When you practice kindness, peace, and love to all, you are living a Lightworker's life.

Sent with peace.
Sent with light.
Sent with love.

I don't know what I'd do without my daughter and her family. Every time I have a crisis, whether good or bad, they come in the door with a smile or a laugh, and tools in their hands to fix it.

I did a thing about two weeks ago, and finally decided to get a new table and chairs for the kitchen area. I'd been using my mother's set for years, and my daughter had used them before me...and Mother had used them for a good thirty years before that. So...going on fifty years of our fat butts in those chairs, and a lot of scooting back and forth, and they need to move along to someone else. The chairs had even been glued back together twice that I know of, and so I gladly turned them over to Habitat for Humanity for another little repair, before they put them out for resale.

My Mother would approve of them being passed on.

But what I ordered came in boxes and had to be put together.

They were delivered a few days ago - and I roll my eyes when I say 'delivered' because FedEx just dumped three big boxes on my front porch, and drove away without even ringing a doorbell. I guess the driver was afraid I might want them carried into the house.

So I had to call my grandson to get them off the front porch. Thank goodness it was still Spring Break, and Scout was home. He put them in the garage for me, and today, my son-in-law came over, took the old table apart and moved it and the chairs into the garage for Habitat to pick up, then he put my new table together.

He's coming tomorrow to put the chairs together, and I'll be good to go. I kept the captain's chair from my mother's set for sentimental reasons, and donated the rest. And life goes on.

. . .

I told you this rather rambling, and lengthy story, as an example of letting go.

It's hard to let go of the past, but often, the only way forward, is to let go of where you were, to get to where you need to be.

The little chair I kept is symbolic of where I've been, but in no way does it hold me back from accepting changes.

The new stuff is symbolic of where I'm going.

Was it hard for me to do this?

No. It was time.

It's time for all of us to let go so we can move up and onward.

Think about a change you could make in your life that would be an uplifting moment. It doesn't have to be a physical change. But nothing grows without evolving...and to live the best life you can while you're here...you must continue to grow your soul.

Remember to share kindness.

Remember to live in a state of gratitude.

Remember to love one another.

*

I learned to sew on my Grand's treadle Singer sewing machine when I was six.

Mother bought a portable electric tabletop machine when I was 9, and I branched out from hemming handkerchiefs, to making aprons in 4-H club.

I cooked on a gas stove for the first time when I was ten. That was also the year I began digging up my own red worms and grub worms for fish bait, baiting my own hook, and cleaning the fish that I caught. I knew how to plant garden, how to make straight rows, which seeds to plant first, and mowed the yard with our old push mower.

Every Saturday morning after breakfast, we cleaned house from top to bottom, and then started laundry. We hung it on a line outside to dry. I ran barefoot from May until sometime in September, and the only time I wore shoes was when we went to town or to church.

I made my own clothes from the age of eleven. That was also the year Daddy taught me how to drive. He put me behind the wheel of our old pickup with a four in the floor gear shift, showed me the clutch, the accelerator, and the brake. He told me what they were for, and to put it in first gear and try not to pop the clutch.

At that point, we began loading up bales of prairie hay. I drove up beside the bales, and Daddy threw them in the back of the pickup. We did that over and over that hot summer day until the field was clear.

I became a full-fledged field hand that day, and every year after until I went away to school. When Daddy began working swing shifts, my sister and I would be up by five a.m. milking cows before school. We were always feeding out a hog to butcher, too.

One summer I outgrew my mother by three inches. I was fourteen years old.

Life was never easy, but it was the only life I knew, and I treasured every moment of that home, and the family into which I was born.

I would never have dreamed back then that I would become a well-known writer. I didn't know life had purpose beyond that small world in which I was nurtured. But that work ethic, and that never-quit attitude, is also what got me where I am today.

I don't quit, and I don't like being told no. I will find a way around whatever is blocking my path, and I will do what I came here to do. It's called living a purpose-filled life.

Back then my purpose was driven by our family life-style.

Now, I am led to share my life and its purpose.

Every day of my life now is to be the messenger for you.

It is my path to heed Spirit's warning, words of praise, or urgent messages of the change that is upon us, and pass them on to you.

Every morning when I wake, my first thoughts are of what Spirit wants you to know.

You are what I think of before I am even dressed. Before a bite of food has gone into my mouth.

You matter to Spirit, and you matter to me.

I can't tell you how to live. It is no one's business but yours.

I share with you what I am told, and I share with you, the light that is within me.

Spirit says:
You have the power to create the world within you.
Be at peace with yourself.
Live in a state of quiet consciousness, knowing that your small moments of joy raise the energy of this world to a better place.
Live with the thoughts of all humanity as being as important.
You are Love.
You are Light.
You are Joy.
Know it.
Live it.

Sometimes I just want to take people by the shoulders and shake them until they look me in the eyes, and listen to the message they were given.

But I don't. I never will. Because as hard as it is for some people to understand, we're all here at different levels of learning and abilities.

What I learned a thousand years ago in other lifetimes, isn't even on someone else's radar here. They're not ready for it, and won't be in this lifetime, and that's okay.

That's where patience comes into play for me - something I continue to work on.

I saw a wild turkey crossing the highway in front of me as I was running and errand for my daughter today, and it made me cry. They remind me of the home Bobby and I shared...watching the huge flocks of wild turkeys coming out from the woods in the evening. They fed among the horses grazing in the pasture, and sometimes, so did a small herd of deer.

I cried because that life is so ingrained in me, that the sight of something wild was felt as a loss.

I struggle daily with living in a city. I have never felt as isolated in my life among so many people.

I just don't belong here.

But here, I am, and so I cope, because that's what you do when life takes you where you didn't plan to go.

Be at peace with where and who you are.

God does not see the physical side of us. Ever.

He knows us, because He sees us as part of The Whole.

As part of Him.

It is particularly important, I think, to live in a way while we are here, so that we do not bring shame upon His name.

We cannot call ourselves a child of God, unless we honor the one true rule...

"Do unto others, as you would have them do unto you."

ଛ

Spirit says the people who need this will see it. It is then up to them what they do with it. So don't comment about it to me. I am only the messenger.

. . .

Free will moves us from one place to another in life. We either stay or leave, according to our free will.

Personal choices are not forced upon us, and using them as a reason why you are personally unhappy is just an excuse.

If your life is a mess...personal choices put you there. Other people may have had a hand in it, but you stayed.

Own your mistakes.

If you continue to blame everyone else for why you are unhappy, you will never see the way out of what's wrong.

You are responsible for your problems, and until you own that and stop blaming others for your failures, your life will never change.

You will sabotage yourself over and over, because you can't believe this good job will last. You got a raise, and are immediately suspicious of how long this good time will last.

You expect to fail, therefore you do.

I say it time and time again, but until you get it, Spirit will keep repeating it.

What you give out into the Universe, you will get back.

If you rage and curse another, it comes back on you ten-fold.

And so it goes.

Whatever you're feeling - whoever you're blaming - stop it.

Stop it now and own what is yours.

God loves you. Friends and family love you. But until you learn to love yourself, you will not grow your financial situation, your happiness, or your life.

Sent with peace.
  Sent with light.
  Sent with love.

I'm going to get a massage this morning, and my back thanks me.

It isn't for luxury sake. It's part of me taking care of me.

There isn't one place on it that doesn't hurt.

I think I'm channeling my daughter's pain, and it wouldn't be the first time. She has four titanium rods in her back, from her neck to her tailbone, and twenty-eight metal screws that hold them in place. She's a walking miracle, and that's a fact.

I don't know how she teaches a room full of rowdy second-graders every day, with that much disability, but she does.

Like she says, "I do what I have to do...what I love to do."

Maybe if I get a massage to relieve some of the ache temporarily, it will help her, too. Being an empath sucks. I feel her pain. We'll see if she can feel my relief. We'll see how this works. I've hurt for a week, and haven't said a word to her about it, but every day when I talk to her after work, she's either lying down on a heating pad, or has ice on herself somewhere, or she's cooking for her family, or chasing their three dogs, or grading papers. I hope this helps her as much as it's going to help me.

In the past two weeks, I've been standing in line to pay for something, and stood there so long I got fed up, dropped everything on a display table, and walked out. What I discovered later was that I didn't really have to have what I was going to buy after all, because I went home, and went back to work without missing them.

This whole world revolves around standing in lines - waiting to be served - waiting to be helped - waiting at someone else's pleasure. I refuse to be a slave to standing in line. I'd rather just go home and forget about it.

I have also been known to do the same thing after being kept waiting more than an hour in a doctor's office. I went up to the receptionist and told her I'm not waiting any longer. When she asked me if I wanted to reschedule, I said, "No, I'm not coming back on another day to repeat this process all over again. I'm going home. I'll either get better or I'll die." And I left.

And I obviously survived to tell the tale.

Patience was always something I struggled with, and the older I get, the less patience I have for the lack of common courtesy. Hire more cashiers. Stop overbooking medical appointments. Those are the two that are most aggravating to me, and yet that's how the world works these days. They're afraid they're going to miss a dollar, so they put things on sale to get in more customers, and then can't serve them promptly, and overbook appointments, then make people wait.

The thing is...I am my own woman, and I'm not about to be herded into compliance, just because everyone else is doing it.

Making your own decisions, however small, is the first step in ridding yourself of frustration and depression. When you feel as if life is out of your control, and you are spiraling without direction, remember it is your life, your path, and your decisions to make.

❧

Talent is what you came with...not what's learned. It's that innate part of you that comes with your DNA.

Many people are skilled at their jobs, and have a sense of what looks right and what doesn't. Talent is that little extra touch that takes something from good to great. Like making good biscuits, or biscuits that melt in your mouth. Like knowing what's wrong with a car engine by the sound. Knowing when someone is suffering, even though they haven't said a word. Taking a painting from pretty, to ethereal.

Talent is instinctive, and we all have a talent.

Some people don't acknowledge their gift.

Others don't recognize that they have it.

Today is a day for analyzing yourself and making use of the gift God gave you.

It's why you came.

***

Yard guy is coming to mow my dandelions and hen bit this morning because that's all the green that's in my yard to mow. But when you live in an HOA you mow.

I remember looking out across my yard out in the country and thinking how pretty it was in early spring. The little white flowers blooming on the wild onions, the tiny grape hyacinths, the bright yellow dandelions, and that purple hen bit - all of them growing together in beauty and harmony.

Plants know how to exist together. Animals have their own hierarchy of existence, but humans cluster in like-minded clumps.

I am not a like-minded clumper. I resist conforming to someone else's opinions. I refuse to be judged or frowned upon because of how I love, and believe, and live my life.

In my heart, wildflowers grow in abundance.

In my heart, kindness is the rule of the land.

In my heart, judgment is left to God.

In my heart, I am allowed to make my own choices.

And so I do...because my heart is my compass.

I choose Light.

I choose Love.

***

It is a cold, rainy morning here.

I am safe, sheltered, and fed, and I am grateful.

But my gratitude would grow exponentially knowing everyone on earth could say the same.

I am certain my empathy for the homeless comes from the lifetimes when I had no shelter. I am certain my empathy for those who are now being judged because of skin color, race, and religion comes from when I was living lives with just those same trials and dangers. Lives when I did not have enough food. When I was on the run from danger, just trying to stay alive.

I must have remembered from those lifetimes, how the kindness of another mattered when I was given food and shelter, or when I was loved regardless of where I was born and what I looked like.

I am certain that's why these things matter to me so deeply now...because I remembered the lessons of suffering and deprivation...the lessons of finding my own strength and of knowing that, in that lifetime, I'd gone there to fail so that I might grow my empathy for those in that situation.

Spirit says:
A true lesson is learned from life experience, not from a book.
Until you have physically and emotionally experienced an event, you will never understand the true depth of what just happened.
You can empathize with the destruction of a storm...of the death of strangers. You can empathize and be angry from the injustice that others are experiencing - but until you have been in those shoes, you can NEVER truly understand.

This is why it's so important not to belittle the rage of others.
This is why it's so important not to condescend and say you understand....when all that's needed are the words, "I am so sorry that you have suffered this."
You cannot insert what you believe is rational thinking, when you're standing on a mountain, safely out of danger while watching people dying in a flood that's down below.

Stop trying to be in charge.

Everyone is where they are because of their own choices...some of which were made in spirit, before their soul contract was even agreed upon.

Walk your own path and pray for your own strength, Pray for others out of love, not from the desire to lay your own wishes for them, above what they have personally chosen.

And so it is.

Joyful morning listening to Sundance Head's new album...Stained Glass and Neon.

For all the fans of The Voice, you might remember him. He was on Blake Shelton's team, and won The Voice a couple of years ago. Yes, he's country, but this is me, remember.

I enjoy most kinds of music, but I LOVE country, because the songs tell stories, and I'm a storyteller. And that's how I roll.

Went to the dermatologist on Friday and had a few spots frozen on my face, and now I'm sporting a blister on my upper lip, a spot on my cheek, and spots on both sides of my head up close to my eyebrows.

That's seventy-five years of sunlight on me, about fifty of which were long before anyone thought about sun being harmful, or knowing that years of sunburns will leave lasting trails of trouble on your skin.

I have always grieved my pale, white skin, and being marked by my mother's French and Irish DNA, and not my Daddy's Cree and Cherokee heritage, even though they are both within me. If I could choose, I would have been as brown as my Bobby. That's the color that is most beautiful in my eyes.

But, I also remind myself that long before I came into this lifetime, I chose my appearance and purpose for a reason.

I used to roll my eyes at the knowledge, wondering why in the world I chose to be someone who could gain weight just thinking about a doughnut.

Was I going down some checklist, marking off the physical description like checking off items on a grocery list?

Why, in the name of chocolate fudge did I think it would be interesting to battle a lifetime of fat?

OR? Was that weight the wall I needed between my soul and humanity, to feel safe? There's always a reason for who and what we become, and I long ago quit bemoaning my appearance.

I know how we walk in life is far more important than how we look when we're living it.

Live your truth.

Love yourself as you love the God-light within you.

And Love one another.

No more.

No less.

I'll be on the road today.

It's raining...and supposed to rain off and on all day. But it's not storms. And it's not snow or ice, so I'm good to go.

I'm really looking forward to meeting everyone at the Friends of the Library fundraiser in Tecumseh today.

And for all you non-Oklahomans, the town Tecumseh is named after Tecumseh, a great war chief of the Shawnee Tribe, and is just south of the city of Shawnee.

Quite fitting, right?

. . .

On rainy days when I was little, Mother made quilt forts for Diane and me. She'd throw a big quilt over the kitchen table and oh my lord, the fun we'd have crawling in and out of our makeshift cave.

We were little animals. We were explorers. We were hiding. We were digging for gold. We were playing house. There was no end to our imagination. A couple of times during the day of the downpour, little snacks would suddenly appear at the door of our cave. Sometimes saltine crackers with little bits of cheese. Sometimes some raisins in a little bowl. And the moment the food arrived, the game changed. It then became about being rescued from starvation at the last moment.

Mother was so patient, ignoring the noise in her kitchen, and working around us as we played.

But the day that started out to be a bummer because we couldn't go outside and play turned into the best day ever.

It was always that way with Mother.

If we were sick, she sat and read stories to us as we would fall asleep, or wrapped us up in that same quilt, and rocked us.

She made us soup, or pudding, and sat beside us when our fevers rose, and wiped our sweaty faces when it finally broke.

Spirit says:

Rain feeds the earth...but it also feeds the souls of the people on it, giving us time to retreat and renew, slowing down the pace of our lives just enough to step back and appreciate what really matters when life storms roll in.

Food. Shelter. Love.

Spirit says:

A building someone calls a church is not a connection to God, and it is not a portal to heaven.

It is a building where people of like minds gather to talk about God.

Talking is good.

Doing and living His Word is better.

A man reading from the Bible is not God.

He is interpreting the words in his own understanding and beliefs, for the people listening.

I don't need to sit in a building to be close to my God.

He is with me always. In every moment of my day, He is witnessing how I live, and what I do, and what I say, not caring how many times I say Amen inside a building.

I am an intelligent woman. I know how to research and seek truths. I will interpret the words in the Holy Bible for myself.

No one but God will tell me how to live my life.

No man is in control of me.

Nobody on earth has power over me, because I am light, and I am part of God's light.

HE IS the power.

My body can be abused.

My heart will one day stop beating.

But I will never die.

And I will have stayed true to the great I AM, because I came, and I followed His rule.

Love others as I have loved you.

Do unto others as you would have them do unto you.

It's that simple, people.

ಶ

Spirit says:

Comfort is the quiet voice in your ear telling you everything is going to be all right. Even when you're in a crisis and you know it's not going to be all right, may never be all right in the same way again.

That voice. That person's love and caring for your fear and heartaches is also love from God.

I can remember when I was little, sitting outside in my swing, flying back and forth into the air as high as I could make myself go, and looking up through the limbs, and the leaves, for glimpses of blue sky. I talked to myself in that swing. I talked to God there. And I cried there. It was my special place to be alone. It was my comfort.

Even as a child I knew that finding time-out for me was crucial. When the fighting inside my house got loud, when Daddy was drunk, and Mother was crying - when Diane was throwing up from crying so hard in the midst of the stress, and her fear of the fighting, I had to remove myself from it to survive it.

We learn to cope with what is, until we can find a way to get out of it...then it becomes what was. It's no longer a factor in our life. The trick is not to live your life as that victim. Yes, you saw it and lived it, but the past never defines who you can become.

Using what has happened to you as an excuse not to move forward, is choosing to live your life as a victim. When you do that, everyone you meet becomes a potential enemy. You see yourself as unable to thrive, because you didn't back then, so there is no way now that you'll ever get ahead. How could you? You're the victim. Remember?

Don't let the past be your present, or you'll never have a future. Don't let your life become a rerun.

You are loved. Feel it.

You are light. Shine it.

You are part of God. Let the world know it in every word you speak and every action that you take.

You are not a victim.

You are a blessing.

❧

You see a fire in the distance...but you didn't set it and so you look away.

Not my fault. Not my business, you say.

You see a flood happening in another part of the country, and you might say a prayer for those in danger, but then you let it go.

I'm not in danger. Everything of mine is safe, you say.

You see bad things happening, but you look away because you don't want to be involved.

Not happening to me. Not going to get involved, you say.

So when do you say enough is enough? When it happens to you? When you're the one who's finally impacted? Is that when you start shouting, 'Danger!" Is that when you go for help? When you have to suffer the pain...when you have to bury people you love?

This isn't about fighting and marching.

This is about not looking away. This is about standing up for truth, not choosing which side will put more wealth in your pocket.

If you admire power over peace - If you are wholly focused on how much wealth you can accumulate, and choose to look away from the unspeakable acts against humanity being committed every day, then understand the time is coming when you will be faced with the cost of your choices.

When you chose to align yourself with the dark side, you became part of the imminent destruction of thousands of years of a world-dominant oligarchy. It is crumbling as I write - coming apart from within and without.

When that fall happens, the world as we have known it for centuries will be forever changed. What was, will no longer exist, and you will have waited too long to change sides.

Put aside your lust for more money, and your admiration of power over peace, for one day. Stop now. Look around you, and understand that it's not just change that's happening...it's destruction.

An old world is dying. A new world is waiting.

It's no longer just about YOU.

It's about US.

Changing lives envelopes the whole of humanity. Not a chosen few.

You can no longer ignore what's coming undone around you.

Choose to love people, not things.

Choose to be kind, not harsh.

Choose to see.

Choose to love.

Choose to change.

ঞ

When my grandchildren and my great-nieces were little, I used to make them little rabbit cakes at Easter, and color coconut in different colors to sprinkle over the icing. They had fluffy little white icing tails, and long ears I cut out of white paper. With six little girls, and then later the one grandson to come along, there were little rabbits all over my kitchen. It was my joy.

I miss making rabbit cakes. I miss my family. But children grow up and go their own separate ways, and that's how it's supposed to be. It does not, however, destroy my memories of that joy.

Life is not about dwelling on losses. It's about rejoicing in the fact that you are still here to experience it. As the only member of my immediate family who is still living, I have always felt a duty to wring all the good I can out of a day before I crawl in bed, because I'm still here, living life for all of us.

It's harder to find things to look forward to, but I refuse to quit on life...even when it's felt like life quit on me.

I didn't want to be here alone. Without my Bobby. Without my sister. Without the anchor of their presence. I knew growing up, that one day I'd lose my parents, but I never thought about losing everyone else, too, except it happened - just like it's happened to so many of you.

So when it happens, you deal with it. That's when you suck it up and find a new way to be in the world. Remember people with love, but don't live in the grief of the day you lost them. Live in thankfulness that they were ever in your life.

Spring is about renewal.

Make a pledge to yourself that this is the day I begin looking at life as a blessing. Put away the altars you have erected to the past, and let it go.

Bring out the pretty things you save for special occasions, and start using them.

You're a special person.

Celebrate you and your life every day.

Celebrate you.

Spirit says:

When the people of Earth weep as loudly for the absence of decency and humanity, as they do for the loss of a structure, then we will have reached the level of being that is pleasing in God's eyes.

Humane is benevolence, compassion, empathy.

People talk about being humane to animals, but that word is rarely used within the reference to human beings, and with obvious good reason.

People war with each other.

Or fight with each other.

Or argue with each other.

They can't live next door to each other in peace.

They won't allow for individuality.

The comfort people find in being with others who look and think like them is fear-based.

Your choices are your choices, but you do not have the freedom to choose for others. It would be in your best interests to stop criticizing other people about what they do, and don't do, with their lives - even to the point of being critical of how they spend their own money - and chastising people who have a lot of it on what they should be doing with it.

God said there should be no other idols before Him, but we have made money our God, and set aside love for our fellowman, to accumulate all that is within our reach.

Spirit says:

God is saddened by the hardness of our hearts.

Be at peace with the uniqueness of others.

Love each other as brothers and sisters.

Structures can be rebuilt, but you can never rebuild a human life.

History is always lost with the passing of time.

But losing a heartbeat is a final and immediate loss of life.

Be thoughtful with which you chose to honor most.

Sent with peace.

Sent with light.
Sent with love.

───※───

People live in a world of constant noise, bombarded from every direction all day long by a cacophony of cars, horns, sirens, people's voices, social media, fighting, gunshots, screaming, shouting, entertainment venues---gathering together for sport and the roar of the crowds, gathering in entertainment venues for the ear-shattering blasts of music from giant amplifiers.

Everywhere they go, there is noise, noise, noise, and at night when they finally go home, the televisions come on, the ear-buds go in, and they are blasting their brains with more, more, more. And all that while, the brain has been sorting and filing the data from the day, verging on overload from it all, with no respite.

The brain is a wonderful computer, but like all computers, if the person does not have the discernment to know the difference between what's true and what's false, if they don't do their own 'find or search' for truths - then the lies they read and believe become viruses in their brains, like the viruses that are downloaded in computers by hackers.

In your brain, a lie that you believe becomes a hack. Your ability to comprehend, has been downloaded with your very own computer virus.

And now that you have accepted it, no amount of talking or explaining from other people can change your minds, because you infected yourself by accepting the lie on face value.

You need to shut down before you can reload.

The best way to find your sanity and your center, is within solitude and silence. Wherever you can find it.

It is an uncomfortable feeling for people who are addicted to technology. They don't know how to be still - to fold their hands in their laps and close their eyes.

It takes a while, and some degree of practice, to remember how to hear their own voices. They heard them when they were children, pretending as they played, but losing imagination is sad.

Substituting it with programmed technology is dangerous.

We have become conditioned to believing the voice over the loudspeaker. What we are told becomes our truth, and we ignore what we personally witnessed or heard.

We let someone else decipher our own experience for us, and it's turned us into little robots, doing what we're told.

There is a verse in Psalms 46:10.

"Be still, and know that I am God."

It is a message to all of us.

Be still in your heart and in your soul so that you might discern the wheat from the chaff...the truth from the lies.

Spirit says:

The toll of regret, and the grief it brings to you, can cause just as many health problems as an actual disease.

We know the side effects of disease come in many forms. From the treatments, to the medicines and their side effects, to the actual impact of the disease, itself.

However, the regret and depression you may be suffering from something you have said, or something you caused to happen that also impacted others, can be treated in a simpler manner.

All it takes is reaching out to those involved, then saying "I'm sorry", and expressing your regret.

After that, the burden is no longer on you.

You have offered peace.

Whether they choose to accept it or not is now their problem...which may become their regret later on if they turn away.

WHEN SPIRIT SPEAKS

. . .

Do you see....in this way...how life works in full circle moments?

You spoke when you should have stayed silent. You spoke again to express your regret. You expressed your love in this way. Your full circle moment is done.

Now they, who felt they had been wronged, have just received the apology they needed. But if they do not accept, then they have to live out their own issues with breaking their own good karma. They got what they desired, and then didn't accept it.

This is a simplistic example of how life works, but Spirit wanted you to see, and to understand, how easy it is to live in peace with each other.

This morning, when I heard the words "The toll of regret and grief," pop into my head, I knew it was meant for you. I type as fast as I can to keep it flowing through me, and I do this each morning for you.

If you take this lightly, then so be it.

But if you understand, and take this into your heart as a way to shift your life into one of gratitude, then you were the ones meant to hear it.

Be at peace.

Love one another.

Live in light.

❧

Just got back from Red Robin after having lunch with my niece. I made her a cherry cheese pie, and sent it home with her when we parted company. She wasn't at my house Easter Sunday, and it's tradition that I make her one at least a couple of times a year.

. . .

Tradition matters greatly to me. It represents the full circle of family in every way. When I was growing up, we always helped each other during harvests and canning season. We worked together, and took home the fruits of our labor, but the work was always shared.

To this day, I use recipes from my Grand, and from Mother, that were written on old lined tablet paper, in their own handwriting, and know I am touching part of my past.

I use the antique dishes I have inherited from them to serve food at family gatherings, and every time I do that, I know that they are with us at the table.

Last Sunday was Easter, and as I looked down the dinner table at all those who had gathered with me, I thought of the days when I would no longer be with them.

I looked at my grandson, and thought one day he will be the father at his own table - then at my great-nieces, imagining their lives as they mature. They're already focusing on their lifework, and I am so proud of all of them.

I looked at my daughter and her husband, and my heart filled with so much love for how they have created their family, and how loving and caring they are toward me. Always making sure I'm cared for if the need arises....always coming to my rescue.

My grandson comes every week and pulls my trash can to the curb for pickup the next morning. My daughter makes me special treats. My son-in-law is my go-to repair and fix-it man. And at the same time, I am the backup for whatever help it is they need.

It's how my family always was when I was little, and I would not have my own family treated any other way. You have each other's back. You call them. You care for them and about them.

Tradition runs deep in all of us. We don't hurt each other. Even if we're on different wave lengths sometimes, it doesn't change the love.

That is how life is supposed to work. I know it's not everyone's story, but it is the right way for family to be.

The good way.

The way that does no harm.

Even if you did not have this in your life before, there is no reason that it cannot be how your life is now.

It is the elder's task to be the hub of a family, and when that elder is gone, another must take it upon himself or herself to step up. It is how tradition works, and it's how it lives on...long after the people who made your childhood special have gone home.

Spirit wants you to know this is a day to be gentle with one another.

The healing, loving energy of the Universe is strong within you, but you must acknowledge the presence, and ask for it to come in.

Spirit never interferes with your free will, so you have to remember to ask for intercession of any kind, and then you have done all you need to do.

Understand that your answers will come.

Maybe not in the way you asked, but an answer is always given.

Spirit always wants you to remember that life on Earth is like school, and while you are here, hard times are your lessons, and joyous times are recess. Neither lasts forever and everything evolves.

Be at peace with all of it and remember - as a soul, you knew and agreed to all of this before you came.

. . .

I can't tell you why you chose the path you're on, but I can promise you that it's true. Even the sad times. Even the hard times. Even through all of that, there is a lesson you sought, and empathy you desired to grow, and understanding that you wished to achieve.

You shout at me now - screaming out in pain. "I did not wish for my loved one to die! I did not wish for this disaster to befall me!" What you have to remember is that as we come here, we may also have AGREED to stand witness to other souls' journeys, which means their deaths or their disasters, by which you have become impacted, are not yours. It is theirs. And you, as a pure and loving piece of God's eternal light, agreed to stand witness, even with a breaking heart, because that's how life on Earth works.

Our job throughout all of it is to be one with Peace, Love, Kindness and Gratitude.

So today...I wish you Love.

And to be gentle with one another in the name of the great I AM.

This is Spirit's message for you.

Even if you speak the right words, and do the right things in public, and you donate, and you sacrifice your time and energy to all the right organizations, God still knows your heart.

He hears the jokes you make in private with others that are racially motivated. He knows you secretly disdain other religions, and he knows you feel holier than other people for how you believe. He knows you have judged others and deem them as "going to hell" because they do not believe as you do. He knows you for the deceiver that you are, because those aren't God's teachings. Those are man's twisted beliefs.

So here's how that deception works.

You might as well be throwing rotten eggs at people now, and speaking aloud the bitter truth in your hearts for all to see, because if God sees your truth, so does humanity.

You fool no one, and you're shaming yourself.

God is the creator of life. All life. He created diversity because it is beautiful in His eyes. Every time you belittle one of God's children, you are shaming yourself. You cannot speak pretty words, and hide your ugly thoughts from Him. Ever.

So why don't you just stop it now? Admit you aren't living the God-filled life you proclaim to be, and start over. Now. With an apology to God, and a prayer for forgiveness.

And after that, just stop the racial rhetoric, and judgment of who's worthy and who's not.

That's not your job.

God created.

God gave.

God loves.

It would behoove you to follow in His footsteps, instead of stomping around in the deep ruts of the narrow-minded choices you have been calling life.

If you yearn for a better world in which to live, then know it begins with you, and the ONLY thing that will make life on Earth better is Love.

God's universal message - the one He first gave that has yet to be followed, still stands.

"Love one another, as I have loved you."

That's the beginning, the middle, and the end of His request.

Follow it.

Do it.

Be the love.

Pray love.

And so it is.

It is our duty as we become parents to set examples for how we want our children to grow up - without deceit, without lies, without prejudice.

By being the living examples of kindness and honor, they will assume this is the natural order of things, and they will automatically copy these behaviors.

As they grow up, they will become influenced by what they see, by their friends, and by life.

If they hear prejudice through your jokes, or hear you laugh about it within the privacy of your own home...if they hear both parents speaking to each other, using harsh, ugly words...and see them fighting rather than sitting down and rationally discussing a situation...they will echo that same behavior back to you and to their peers. And using the excuse that you are the adult, and for them to do what you say, when they've seen you do the opposite, isn't ever going to work.

The one thing children come here with is the instinct to be fair and honest. They LEARN deceit from what they see and hear.

This is why it is so important to continue to talk about what's happening in the world to them, and explain your viewpoint...of how sorry you are it is happening, about how mean and thoughtless it was of people to belittle someone who has less, and the dangers that can happen when you're not aware.

The world in which we grew up in, and the one in which we raised our children, no longer exists. This world is a mine field of dangers for children.

In this way, if they are already practicing any of the negative behaviors, you are still schooling them with your feelings and emotions, without attacking them face on.

And if you do this from the beginning - when they first start to school and come home talking about who did what during the day, and you know they will talk about it then, this is the time in which these lessons begin, and they must continue throughout their growing up years.

If you leave your children to their own devices, and if you do not communicate to them beyond demanding and arguing about things they haven't done at home, they are never going to talk to you about what is happening when they are away from home.

The old saying - it all begins at home - will always hold true.

It is not the teacher's responsibility to teach children morals.

It is not the law's responsibility to pull your children in line.

But it will become the court's responsibility to enact punishment.

And it will become the undertaker's responsibility to bury them when you are bereft with grief, and wondering how they got into such trouble, and with disbelief that all of this happened.

It happened because you didn't honor the law of nature. The one that animals follow better than man. Do not abandon your children to the care of others.

Do not ignore where they are going, or what they do.

In this time, in this world, no child is safe, and you all know it, because you constantly post the messages with missing children.

Raise them kind, but raise them wise.

You can't shield them from danger.

But you can teach them how to avoid it.

Sent with peace.
    Sent with light.
    Sent with love.

Once upon the time when the Earth was new, God asked..."Who in my Universe will volunteer to go to this new place to be caretakers of the land, the water, the air, the plants and the animals upon it?"

And the Star Beings said, "We will do it, because we look down upon all that is beyond us, and when we are there, we will be able to look up and see home."

And so God was pleased, and the Star Beings came down and took human form and created their shelters, and honored Mother Earth and The Great Spirit, and learned the ways of the plants, and honored the animals they took as food, thanking them for the sacrifice of their spirit, and promising not to waste any part of the animal in the taking.

And so it was...

And Earth thrived, and the waters ran clean and pure, and the animals flourished, and the plants healed them, and it was as God wished.

This is the beginning of the journey of indigenous peoples of this earth. They were always meant to keep the knowledge of the spiritual plane that exists between man and heaven. And they have tried.

Only God, knows how hard they have tried throughout history, even when they were slaughtered in great numbers. Even when they were displaced because of the greed of others, they never quit on their promise to care for it, and to teach others.

Their purpose when they came was clear. They were not directed to build great cities, and herd people to a place to be ruled by the power of a dynasty, and controlled by fear and starvation.

And because they were gentle people in the beginning, they were easily duped. Only later, did they rise up as nations, and try to defend the land they'd so lovingly tended for centuries.

They are still fighting, but in the courts now, and with mass protests that often end with their injuries and deaths. They tried desperately to save the land, and the plants, and keep the waters clean, and never hunt for trophies only.

But they could not keep up with what white men destroyed, and we did not heed their warnings, because we saw the Star Beings as people who lived in huts, and tepees, and in the rain forests, and in the African jungles, and the American deserts, and in the great mountains of Nepal, and the islands of Australia, and New Zealand.

Those people tried to tell us, but they were judged by the color of their skin, and the lack of amenities in which they lived. We didn't acknowledge the spiritual connections they had with God, because of how they looked, and where they lived. We didn't understand that, as keepers of the Earth, they chose to live with it, and within it, and we did not, and this is why Mother Earth is dying.

Today, I honor all of the indigenous peoples of Mother Earth for your valiant efforts, and when the day of your ascension finally comes, you will return to the stars with your promises to God complete.

Spirit says:
Challenge yourself today to be humble in all you receive and all you do.

Acknowledge your worth by your service to others.

Don't seek the tasks with prizes.

Seek the ways in which you can make a difference.

It is an important a step to growing your light and energy, as rain and sunshine are to growing things.

Let go of ego.

Be a part of humanity, not apart from it.

Without knowing it, we infect others with the broken parts of ourselves. What was done to us, we do to others.

I read once where someone said..."No one gave me anything. I had to work for everything I have. Yes, I am in debt, but if I'm in debt, then it's only fair that everyone is in debt."

Every day we work toward a better world, but how can that world exist, when we begrudge a change that brings a better life to others? Do we not consider the future of our children's children? Do we wish strife on all of humanity forever and ever, because it was once so done to us?

This thinking is the root cause of the dis-ease in which we all live, which causes disease to our bodies and darkens our hearts.

Jealousy is a fault.

Coveting that which others have is also breaking a commandment.

You cannot change anything or anyone but yourself.

So today, walk a humble path and see how you feel at the end of the day.

If you feel anxious and unhappy with yourself because no one praised you and your work, you have some work to do on yourself.

You do not need the praise of others to feel satisfied in a job well done.

Be at peace with yourself.

Stand in Light.

Pray Love.

Spirit says:

If there is turmoil in your life, make peace with yourself about how you got there.

If there are apologies you can make, then make them.

If you are holding onto your indignation, because you think someone owes you an apology, let it go.

Forgive them in your heart and it is done.

Life is never about being at war with someone.

If you have put yourself in strife, then it is upon you to get yourself out of it the best way possible, leaving no hard feelings behind.

But by the same token, you cannot force someone to accept your advances for peace. All that matters in your life is that you made them, then move on.

I know people who cannot exist without turmoil. They don't know how to just "be" in the world without enemies, and they need to always be the victims to feel worthy. They don't know any other way to gain attention for themselves except to live in discord, and if their lives are suddenly leveling out and calming down, and there aren't any wars to foster, or gossip to spread, they create it.

A narcissist always has to be at the forefront of importance.
    They can and will create big drama, even to the point of emotionally and physically harming others, and then find a way to turn the blame onto the people they hurt, which then gives them, the narcissists, the opportunity to fall apart in despair at how terrible life is treating them. They destroy the people who love them. They are master manipulators, and thrive on discord.

It is upon you to find the place you feel most comfortable, and then work to stay in a place of peace with yourself, and with the people in your inner circle.
    If all you manage to do in this life is fight, then you will be back, again, and again, and again, until you remember why you're here, and finally fulfill the soul contract you made before you came.

Sent with peace.
    Sent with light.
    Sent with love.

For everyone who has complained and griped about immigrants coming across the Rio Grand, etc., etc., etc., I am going to assume those Cinco de Mayo parties you usually plan in great detail will no longer be a part of your social calendar. Unless of course, you are giving yourself a one-day detente with hating Mexicans, just so you can party.

And YES this is meant to be sarcastic.

And NO, this isn't a political post.

Call it my version of an Andy Borowitz piece.

As a descendant of a two Native American tribes, and a whole butt load of European immigrants, I am permanently incensed at all of the hate in this country regarding immigrants. Part of my ancestors were original to the continent, and the rest of them were dirt poor, starving immigrants running from oppression, wars, and slaughter,

Oh wait! That sounds familiar, doesn't it?

Never mind.

My Irish and French and English ancestors got off a ship in a port in North America without issue, many at Ellis Island within the shadow of the Statue of Liberty without being turned away, registered their names in a book, and went about their business.

God forbid that we'd ever see the relevance of where we came from, since this country as it exists now, seems to feel it is their privilege to be entitled to be first, and to be right.

I don't care how you convince yourself that you are right about denying dying people a better place to be, you shame yourself in the eyes of God.

⁂

I made a trip home today...and by home, I mean Paden, Oklahoma.

Tonight is the end of school award assembly for Paden High School, where my sister and I graduated.

I had to drop off my scholarship stuff for the student who is getting the Diane Lynn Thompson scholarship that I give to a graduating senior each year in my sister's name.

Then I stopped in Prague, Oklahoma, where I spent most of my married life, on the way home and ate lunch at Cowboy's. As I was getting up to leave, I saw my ex-husband, (my children's father) and his nephew sitting at a booth. I stopped by to say hi, and wound up sitting with them, and visiting for a good thirty minutes.

I left, but only after promising the next time my daughter went home to see her dad, that I'd send my nephew some kolaches. For those of you who don't know this, kolaches are Czech sweet rolls.

I don't know what most of the Sala family thinks about me, and it's not my place to care. He and I have been divorced since 1996, but once I become part of someone else's family, or they become a part of mine, they will always be family to me.

But I'm home now and so glad to be here. No traffic to cope with. Just my old clothes back on, my shoes off, and a glass of iced tea within reach as I type. Life is just about perfect.

It's how I judge the quality of my life. If my family is well, if my feet don't hurt, and I'm snug in my little home being happy, then that is enough.

I can't change what others think about me, but I can change how I think about them. I hold no expectations, no judgments, no grudges. I don't give away my power any more, which is huge for an empath, because it is so easy to fall into the emotional sinkholes of other people's lives.

I am at peace today, and I wish the same for all of you.

Try not to get lost in drama that doesn't belong to you.

It will make all the difference between living a peaceful and purpose-filled life, or one of tension, anger, and turmoil.

. . .

I pray Love and Healing to all of you.
   I pray Love and Healing all over this Earth.
   And so it is.

~

The new day called to me, waking me from a dream of helping people choose.
   I don't like those dreams much, but while I know what they're supposed to pick, I can't interfere with their free will to make their own choices.
   So getting up and out of bed was a good distraction. I make my own choices, whether I'm awake, or if I'm spirit walking, and the consequences fall to me, which is how it should be.

My son-in-law came and removed all of the old flower pots from my back patio. I'm not replanting in them this year, and I don't feel like having pots of anything to water this year. They had all turned into ant colonies anyway.
   It was a painful hassle last year, dragging long garden hoses around the yard, and I tripped over the hose on my patio twice last year, so I'm not going down that road again. Escaped injuries then, only because of my angels, and I'm not taking risks I don't need any more.
   The one fall I took that could have been bad, was because I was still on concrete, beneath the shade of my patio.
   My daughter and son-in-law were there, and I know it scared them. It scared me, too, because I knew my shoulder and head were going to hit the concrete patio...and as I began to fall, I kept thinking... *not the concrete, not the concrete.*

Then the weirdest thing happened. For a couple of seconds, everything froze around me...my daughter's horrified expression...my son-in-law in the act of running toward me. BUT I was still in motion...no longer falling down, but like I was being moved sideways, toward the grass. And that's where I landed. The only thing still on the concrete were my feet. The moment I was down, those seconds of stopping time were over, and my daughter was running toward me, and my son-in-law was already at my feet. They helped me up, made sure I could walk and use all my limbs, that I wasn't bleeding anywhere, etc. But I already knew I was okay, because my angels had lifted me out of harm's way. And they had acted, because my heart called out to them in a moment of need. They can't interfere with free will, but I did not mean to fall. And they can't interfere with my soul contract, but an injury was obviously something I wasn't supposed to endure at that time.

Why am I telling you this? So you'll pay attention in your own life when your angels have intervened for you. The times you've been driving through a city and hit all the red lights, only to drive up on a massive accident a few minutes later. You think, wow, if I'd been a few seconds earlier, I'd be in the middle of that. But you weren't there, because the angels slowed you down. You weren't meant to receive a lesson in that way.

The times you stepped away from someone you didn't trust, and find out later they'd been arrested for something. You call it instinct. I call it listening to my angels.

There are far more unseen miracles and blessings on Earth, than you can ever imagine.

Because you're not aware.
Because you aren't awake.
Because you aren't listening.
Be aware. Be grateful. Always thank them.
I pray Love and Healing all over this Earth.
And so it is.

It rained a slow, gentle rain off and on all night, and is supposed to do the same thing through the day. It's cold out. I have the central heat on, AND my gas fireplace, trying to heat my house. These big twelve and sixteen foot ceilings are a heat trap. Heat rises, which is a good thing in the summer, because it's easier to keep the rest of the house a little cooler, but it's not a good thing in cold weather.

Ah well...everything's a trade-off. To get the good, you also have to put up with some bad. Nothing is perfect, and certainly not the weather.

I have a load of laundry going, I've carried my canned food donation out to the curb for the mailman to pick up...(It's their annual food drive for the food bank) and I have begun my day.

More writing...and then some more writing.

I live such an exciting and glamorous life.

Just like in the movies.

What you see is not real.

What you think is but an illusion.

I wish we were all in a big room together so I could touch you, hug the ones who need it, and hold your hands while I listen to your stories, because everyone deserves to be heard.

I wish you believed what I know.

I wish I could help you understand what is real, and what is not.

If you only knew to just let go of everything you're being told and go be you.

If you only understood how unimportant being part of the in-crowd really is.

If you only understood how close we are to the danger of living in a world controlled by the power of the few, then you would understand why I keep saying this. Why I keep repeating these words:

Let it go. Live in peace. Be kind to everyone of every race and color. Be grateful.

Do Unto others as you would have them do unto you.

. . .

You don't understand your own power to change the world.

If at this moment...right now as you're reading this...every person who's troubled by what's happening in the world suddenly turned loose of hate and revenge, and envy and greed, and opened their hearts to humanity with love and peace for all, the darkness would disappear. Forever.

We would instantly be living in a higher dimension.

Energy is a scientific fact. The vibration of Love is at 528 HZ. That's a scientific fact.

If we loved humanity at that vibration, the dark ones could not exist here and they know it.

So they feed your anger and grow stronger, and you fall into their traps, and shout aloud your rage, and demand "somebody" do something. And the dark ones laugh, because you are the somebody with the power, and you give it away - daily.

So this is what I know.

This is what I wish you understood and practiced.

As for me,

I wish you Joy.

I wish you Peace.

I wish you Love.

I pray Love and Healing all over the people of this Earth.

And so it is.

I went to Walmart about an hour ago to get the rest of the Memorial flowers I needed before they were all gone.

I'd had bad dreams last night, and I am trying to stay in a place of peace today, so being among a crowd of people all doing last minute Mother's Day shopping, was not something I was looking forward to. But it is what it is, and I chose to go.

On the way, I drove up behind a car that had a decal of four white feathers that had the appearance of being blown into a wayward kind of circle, and the word Dream, was beside them.

I reminded God, as I drove, that if that was a message from Spirit for me, it was misplaced. I dream all night, some of which are nightmares that I never mention, and I walk daily in a dream state of waiting for a miracle, rather than sitting in a wake-state, waiting for some apocalypse, and God knows it.

He's heard about my disenchantment with what's left of our Earth. He knows my heart.

So I take my disgruntled self into Walmart, and I'm looking around at what's left of the artificial sprays, etc., and I hear a lady talking, and I think, she's talking to me. I look up, and there is a thin, white-haired woman pushing a walker, and she's trying to tell me about a little boy and his daddy she saw out in the parking lot. The little boy was dressed up like Batman, cape and all, and the daddy was dressed up like Robin. She was so delighted with what she'd seen that she needed to share it, and we spoke, and had a laugh at what a great dad that guy must be.

Then I move to another side of the aisles where there are more flowers, and almost immediately, another very tiny, very elderly lady in a wheelchair, with hair so white it looked like it was glowing beneath the light, rolled up and stopped right beside me.

"Don't forget to water those," she said, and of course I laughed, which she was waiting for, because the flowers were artificial. I told her, "these are the only kinds of flowers I can't kill," which made her eyes twinkle, and off she went.

I finished my shopping and headed home, but I kept thinking about the message to Dream...and the four white feathers, which are signs from angels, and the two tiny white-haired ladies, both of them using aids to walk to remind me I am blessed to be standing on two feet, and I started crying.

God knew I was struggling with this place, and sent me angels to make me smile. I know it as certainly as I know my own name.

So, the message I was sent has been received.

I will still Dream, but just so you know, I'm still looking up, waiting for that ride out of here, too.

※

This is for all of my friends who resent the holiday that is Mother's Day, and take it as their day to wear sackcloth and ashes as a way to tell everybody they're not special. The day to wallow in self-pity for their circumstance.

This post if for the ones who lost mothers when they were young, and have gone through life using that as their reason for being unhappy.

This is for the ones who had mothers who did not show them the kind of love a child needs to be nurtured.

This is for the ones who never knew their mothers, and have used that knowledge to feel unwanted.

Spirit wants you to know this:

Before you ever left heaven, the soul who volunteered to carry you, was there on earth and waiting for your arrival, as she'd promised you she would be.

You were no accident of a night of careless sex.

You weren't given away because you weren't loved.

You didn't lose your mother when you were young as a punishment in any way.

It was a soul contract between the two of you - for whatever purpose your soul wanted to learn here on earth. Maybe to grow empathy...to understand abandonment, to learn forgiveness.

And for the ones of you who were abandoned as babies, or lost your mothers very young, what you don't remember is, that in heaven, you are very, very powerful souls, and that only the very strongest could survive those kinds of beginnings.

You are older souls who desired deeper knowledge - greater understanding of the human condition, and the only way you could know it was to live it.

So today, despite the human your mother turned out to be, honor the soul she is/was who agreed to give you life.

Honor her sacrifice to be hated.

Honor her sacrifice to die young, because it was all done for you.

Not to you.

FOR YOU.

She honored her soul contract, and now it is on you to understand your existence in this way, so that as you finish your earthly journey, everything you came here to learn will be done.

Sent with peace.
    Sent with light.
    Sent with love.

&a.

One political side is posting ugly memes about the other side, and vice versa, most of which are either distorted truths, or flat-out lies, and they don't care as long as it serves their purpose, while the mad fiddler continues a path of destruction, protected by the greed of those in power.

The dark side is in a panic to regain the foothold they had. The curtains are coming down between them and us, and so they feed dissidence into the public information system to keep us in conflict.

The weather has gone crazy. The land has been poisoned. The waters have been fouled. Children die at school. They disappear into the funnel of child trafficking.

Half the people are afraid of their shadows, and the other half wave guns around daring people to take them.

Everyone thinks what they believe is right, so trying to work out problems is never going to happen because no one is willing to listen, let along change.

Part of us know what's happening, and the rest of us will be blind to the truth until we die.

I want to stand on a mountain top, and scream until the sound is heard all over the world, and with my last breath, scream STOP. JUST STOP. But no one is listening. They're all talking over each other in a desperate need to be heard.

The ugliness of this world is breaking my heart.

Everyone of you came here with a pure and perfect soul, who knows better than to do what you're saying and doing. If you won't listen to anybody else, at least listen to your conscience.

If what comes out of your mouth hurts others, then stop it.

If you're involved in criminal activities...walk away.

If you're littering this planet, then quit doing it.

If you're spouting prejudice and racism, go stand in front of a mirror and scream those words at yourself and see how that feels.

If you need a gun in your hand to feel safe, then pray to be released from that fear.

If you can't see your own faults, then look into the faces of the people looking back at you.

If you have made them afraid, you will see it in their eyes.

If you have disgusted them with your words and behavior, you will see it on their faces.

I wish so much for humanity.

My faith in God is pure.

My faith in humanity....not so much.

I have but one message from Spirit today.

STOP THE MADNESS.

CHALLENGES

I have been presented with one today. I prayed to Spirit for help, but this one just means more work...different work...and yet I feel Spirit telling me to do it. So I accepted the challenge.

I still have faith that one of these days I'll be presented with good news that does not involve me and more work.

Oh, I could have said no. But Spirit said, YES, so I heeded the message.

Now will somebody up there heed one of mine? Please?

And as Bobby used to say, TO-DAY!

Expiration dates:

Challenges are assigned lessons, and sometimes, like in the old Mission Impossible stories, they can expire. Not always in sixty seconds, but they will expire. You either decide to accept it, or you don't. And if you don't, then you have to let it go, because second-guessing a decision you've already made is a waste of time. If you want a different outcome later, you'll have to wait for a new opportunity.

Timing:

Time can exist in many different dimensions at the same moment...but since we're only in this one, it's a case of now or never. Other challenges WILL come along later, but the lesson will be different, and so might the outcome.

Trusting:

. . .

This is why trusting your instincts are important. In my life experiences, my first choice was nearly always the best one, which was proven to me later when I did not take it.

This history was what pushed me to accept my challenge today, and we'll see how it goes.

I faced my reluctance.

Recognized my free will.

Accepted the challenge.

And so it is.

※

I'm sleeping in tomorrow, thus the late night post for you guys to wake up to. Yes, I take my duty to Spirit seriously.

Back in the day, there was a song by Mike and the Mechanics called Silent Running. In the song, there's a phrase that goes, "Can you hear me? Can you hear me running? Can you hear me running, can you hear me calling you?"

So that's what Spirit feels like to me. Until I sit down and write to you, the feeling won't go away.

Tell them, Spirit says. Can't you hear me? Sit down and tell them, Spirit says, and so I write.

The rage is high.

Anger is spreading like wildfire across the land.

You can't stomp out the fire with marches.

You can't put out the fire no matter how many tears you shed.

You can't change what was done by threats.

You can't pray it away.

And you can no longer look away.

See what happened when you thought injustice would never touch you.

See what you did when you didn't vote.

See what you did when you let public opinion sway your better judgment.

Look how far you've fallen.

And now you're angry.

Now you care.

Fix it! you cry.

This isn't right! you shout.

It isn't fair, you wail.

What can I do? you ask.

And Spirit says:

If every word you cursed turned into a blessing.

If every fist raised in anger opened up into a hand and linked hands with a stranger.

If every threat you uttered turned into thanks.

If every prayer you prayed for yourself turned into a prayer for someone else, the very air you breathe would be humming from the rise of energy.

It would be impossible to raise a voice in anger, because the darkness it takes to do that would no longer exist.

Put out the fire with Kindness.

Assuage your anger with Peace.

Calm your aching heart with Gratitude.

And pray Love all over this earth and the people on it.

And so it is.

Sent with peace.
Sent with light.
Sent with love.

We are all word weary. Yes, WORD...weary. We've heard too much divisive rhetoric. We all...women and men and children even...feel threatened, but from different things. When that happens, words become weapons, threatening our freedom in every aspect of our lives. Every man isn't wrong, and every woman isn't right, and children are caught in between.

When angry words are spoken, lines are crossed, and ugly truths come to light. We suddenly see people for who they are, and we realize how insecure our place in the world has just become.

This is when new boundaries are made, and old mores are discarded.

Instead of responding with more angry words, show your displeasure in ways that make more sense to the situation.

If it means changing what is familiar to you to feel safe again, then do it. Your other choice is to keep doing what you're doing, and let the wave of inhumanity sweep you under.

There is a parallel happening between our sister women in Mexico, and what's happening to our sister women here now.

Those women have been enduring fear and hardships for generations, trying to exist and keep their families safe amid the power struggles of criminals, until it got so bad that they grabbed their families and ran for help.

We judged them.

We looked away while their children were stolen from them and they were put in jail.

We listened to white men telling us they were evil.

We didn't want their troubles.

We didn't know it was a precursor to the troubles coming to us.

But we do now.

What you didn't see...what you refused to admit was that there were already families here who have been enduring the same thing for generations.

Single mothers trying to keep their families alive while living among drug and gang wars in the projects, and in the slums of every city, and every poverty stricken area of rural America. And we still looked away - until injustice began to strike at the hearts of all women here.

We're having our rights stripped away and it doesn't feel good, does it?

Middle and upper class white women in America are not used to being ignored. They don't like this onslaught to their rights.

But it's here. And whether they like it or not, they are facing now, what their sisters of color were born into.

Women. Here's your sign.
There is no difference among us, save the level of power.
If WORDS are all you have...then accept your fate as done.
Killing each other won't stop this.
Forming groups against each other won't stop this.
But each woman has the power to interfere on her own behalf.
Whatever you're doing FOR men who are doing this TO you, is proving to them that you are worth nothing to them, but a means to their own comfort.
You are making their world comfortable, at the expense of your own.
Think about it. You may even come to understand the desperation of your sister women south of the border.
You don't have to run away to make a point.
You don't have to die to make a point.
Women are not slaves to men.
We all answer to God.
But no man has the power over us, save what we give them.

Spirit says:

Today can be your day of peace and grace, if you make it so. You are always in the driver's seat of your life unless you have given away your power to someone else.

And I say to you, if you have, then remember you have the free will and power to take it back. All you have to do is say, "No More."

But I remind you...being the kind and loving person that I know you are, do remember to thank them for their time and attention to your business, and remind them they'd best get back to tending their own, because their stuff went all to hell while they were focused on you.

That's how you take back your sovereignty.

You just open your mouth and speak it.

Wake up today.

Oh...I see your eyes are open, but you're not seeing your truth.

You're right where you let life put you...in a neat little box. Like being in a house with only one room.

Do you know how to open a door?

Then you know how to get out of that box.

I grew up hearing my Grand say, "pretty is, as pretty does."

I thought she was talking about how someone looked. I had to get older to realize she was talking about actions. That no matter how you looked, it was how you behaved that mattered.

There is a style to being honest and gracious at the same time. You don't have to fight to state your truth. You can say anything you need to say, to anyone you need to say it to, and in a calm and quiet voice. When your words are not spoken in anger, they can easily be heard.

Birth a new you today.
 I showed you the doorway.
 I even opened the door.
 All you have to do is walk over the threshold and out into the New World of possibilities.

❧

My Grand taught me how to embroider and bake yeast breads.
 My Mother taught me how to sew, and how to plant vegetable gardens, and how to can and freeze the produce.
 My Daddy taught me how to fish, and how to clean them, and how to change a flat tire, and what storm clouds looked like that had hail in them. He taught me what milk weed looked like, and that rubbing the white juice on my legs where I'd walked through stinging nettles would make it stop burning.
 My Grampy taught me how to find the ripe watermelons in the patch and where to look for the biggest dewberries. What little patience I have came from him, too.
 My Bobby taught me everything I know about listening - and seeing beyond the obvious. He gave me hope again when I had none. He allowed me to be myself, and loved me without ever once telling me how to walk in this world. He gave me back my power as a woman.
 What you see of me. What I share about myself is such a tiny, tiny part of who I am.

I am a child of the past, but a woman who is given glimpses into the future.

Now think about yourself. Think of all you were, and the tiny bits of your past that make you the person you are today.

Remember the people who were integral parts of your history.

Remember what they gave you...what they taught you.

Think of their presence as the angels passing through the life that was given to you.

They were your examples - your teachers - the people you loved and looked up to.

As you have aged, without being aware of it, you have become the teacher, the example, the angel passing through, sharing what you know with those who are still new to this world.

But be careful of what you share.

Be aware of the seeds you sow in their impressionable minds.

This is where the perpetuation of racial prejudice and religious persecution needs to stop.

This is learned behavior and profiled thinking.

This is a horrible legacy to pass on to another generation.

You can't stop others, but you can stop yourself from turning a precious child into a hateful bully.

People talk about making teachers wear body cams in class so the parents can see how their children are behaving.

This is absurd.

They're your children.

However they behave at home, is what they take to school.

You already know how they behave - exactly how you let them.

You teach them how to be, and then they mirror it to the world.

You have a chance to change the world, but polluting the innocence of the next generation is not how to make that happen.

Be the angel they need you to be.

Sent with peace.

Sent with light.

Sent with love.

※

When I was a little girl, I believed what people said.

I took everything that was said to me as truth, and doubt never entered my mind. I had not yet been betrayed in any way that would lead me to feel unsafe or insecure.

The people who loved me didn't lie to me.

That innocence died as I grew older, but I still hold that as a rule of thumb to the people I let into my world.

Lie to me and we're done.

And I hold grudges.

So there's that.

It's something I've been working on most of my life, but as of yet, it's still part of who I am.

I consider it part of my personal self-defense. It keeps me from repeating the same mistakes with the same people. I will trust you forever until you teach me not to, and then I'll never turn my back on you again.

So how do I relate that broken part of me, into the person who talks about peace and love and light - and how walking away from interfering in other people's battles is how you're supposed to live?

The truth is, we've all been broken, but the trick is to remember you are still here. You survived whatever happened, so don't relive the betrayals over and over. Don't let it become all of who you are.

The best revenge is to be happy.

You can protect yourself in every way you need to feel safe, but don't live in a constant state of fear and distrust.

Find your happy place and grow roots.

If you haven't yet figured out the way to get there, ask the person in the mirror.

The power to be happy is already there.

Sent with peace.
    Sent with light.
    Sent with love.

It's been storming here for a couple of days.

One of the meteorologists just commented they'd been getting complaints at the station, because the bad weather didn't hit in OKC as predicted, and I'm sitting here thinking, What in the name of all that's holy is wrong with people?

You're MAD because you weren't hit by a tornado?

You feel the need to be sarcastic about being safe?

You feel indignant because a cold front has slowed down a massive storm?

Was this just your insecure self feeling the need to tell someone they're wrong?

Well, you're an idiot, so there's that.

You wouldn't know you'd been blessed if Jesus, Himself, was standing in front of you just to prove it was a miracle.

Bless your heart, just hang onto your expectations.

The night isn't over yet.

I've been praying for three straight days that this storm would lose power, or even better, just disappear, and some fool is unhappy that it might happen.

I do heartily apologize for praying away your heart's desire.

I guess this is proof we've had too much rain in this state already, because it's washing fools out from under the rocks where they reside.

Jesus Take The Wheel.

That is all.

Spirit says:

We accumulate many things in life, the most detrimental of which are grudges.

We hold onto them as if they were worth something. As if time would make them more valuable the older they became.

We resurrect them on a regular basis because we believe we're still owed some kind of justice for the slight.

But the strange thing about grudges is their hidden dangers.

They first hurt our feelings, and then the older the grudge, the more hazards they present.

They become emotional infections that seep into every aspect of our life, preventing us from experiencing joy, or from feeling gratitude for anything good.

They affect us physically from everything to headaches, to heartaches, to real physical stress, which then leaches into our spirits. We can't see the good for remembering the bad.

The older the grudge, the deeper the wound.

You will not heal because you won't let go.

If being right is that important to you, then understand that the poor health and hard days ahead of you, are a direct result of your inability to let go - to forgive - and to forget.

Whatever was said or done that enraged you to the point of this emotional fracture, is nothing to what you did to yourself afterward.

Harsh words spoken in the past have no place in your future.

To be at peace, just let it go.

Sent with peace.
    Sent with light.
    Sent with love.

I say to myself:
If only these things were real.

Reset buttons for humans.
    Rooms for adult time-outs.
    A mirror that would show people how they look and act toward others.
    When we're sick, a place where we could go to sleep, and wake up healed.
    Instant empathy for others.
    World-wide abhorrence of war.
    Never going hungry.
    Never having to be afraid.
    No such thing as being homeless.
    Innate care for earth, air, and water.
    Comfort and shelter being a given.
    No such thing as crime.

These are my dreams. My wishes for humanity. My vision of a perfect world. If only I didn't have to dream about them to attain them. If only it was there outside my door.
    You might try holding it together for once and seeing how it feels at the end of the day knowing you didn't make someone cry or hurt their feelings.
    You didn't hate.

You didn't harm.
You didn't steal.
You didn't judge.
You didn't lie.
If only these things were real.

Tornado went through several Oklahoma towns last night, some far too close to me. It also swept through Prague, Oklahoma last night, where I used to live, moving across the place where my ex-husband lives out north of town. It uprooted an old Sycamore tree in the back yard, and fell across a wooden fence in the back yard. I remembered helping dig that tree up from the creek bank and plant it in the back yard forty years ago.

My daughter said her daddy heard the wind, got up and looked out the front door, but didn't see anything. Then, he thought about getting under the stairs and then looked out the back door first, and saw the tree had fallen over and laying on the fence. "Looks like it's over," he said, and went back to bed.

My daughter kept saying..."Oh my God, Mama. We were standing right there yesterday afternoon, and now that stuff is gone. Scary how fast something can end in this world."

Yes, the tree will be cut up for firewood, and the fence can be rebuilt, but as her daddy told her, "If the tree had fallen to the East instead of to the West, it would have landed on me in bed, and I wouldn't be here."

So losing a tree, and a fence, instead of a life, is the best possible outcome for the situation.

The weather we are experiencing is a mirror image of the world in which we live, and that is no coincidence.

I keep saying, "that which you put out into the world, you get back tenfold," and the ugliness and disparity between people right now is beyond my understanding.

I don't have a way to make people see what they're doing to each other, but I do have the power to take myself out of it, and this I do, every day.

I can make powerful changes by living in a place of peace.

I don't take darkness with me.

I do not make others suffer for what I might feel.

Be kind.

Live in a state of gratitude.

Pray Love.

Flowers put out at Prague, Paden, and Arlington cemeteries here in Oklahoma.

Thank God for my daughter who took me. I am so tired and windblown. I didn't remember to fill up with gas before we left, and just now as we drove into the garage, the fuel light dinged. The gauge was on E for Empty.

We looked at each other in shock, then she backed straight out of the garage and drove up the hill to the closest gas station.

My tank holds 16 gallons, and she put 15.05 gallons of gas in the tank.

AND...when she found a penny at the pumps, she laughed and handed it to me. Bobby! Probably thanks to him in some way for getting us home on empty. At the least, he was laughing at us.

The kolaches I made yesterday were delivered today to her daddy and his nephew. Two happy Bohemians for sure.

Her daddy loaded my daughter and I up in his truck, and took us out into the pasture to the Arlington cemetery, which is on his property, so my daughter could put flowers on her aunt Mary's grave. Then we stopped at the house and got my nephew, and we all went to lunch in town.

I'm sure it raises eyebrows now and then, that I have a good relationship with the man I divorced, but I refuse to let other people's ways of living impact what I believe is right. We shared thirty-one years of marriage, and we share two children and four grandchildren, and I will not do that in anger.

I had a couple of teary moments today. Seeing the names of all my people on headstones is a sobering sight.

Being the only one left even more so.

Mother's grave is still red dirt with just a few sprigs of Bermuda grass finally taking hold. She died in November of 2018 during the winter, and grass is just now beginning to grow out here in May of 2019.

The rawness of the sight is somehow just a little bit harsher, as if there was no blanket there to cushion the memory of the loss.

But now I'm home.

The sad is fading, and life goes on.

❧

Spirit says:

When you share the good things you receive, you automatically increase the quotient of good that came from the initial gift.

Last night, I said prayers of Love and Healing for all of you.

This morning, I am sending blessings of gratitude for your friendship and kindness.

As you receive the knowledge of this message and the gifts, so then pass them on.

Be the blessing for someone else this morning by telling them how much you appreciate them as friends.

Be the blessing for someone else this morning by reminding your loved ones how much they mean to you in this life.

They may already know it, but hearing it said aloud spreads it farther.

I tell you over and over how being angry, and fighting with each other only perpetuates the battles.

But if you switch your emotions to the reverse, and speak of gratitude, and live a life of kindness and love, the anger and fighting do not exist. There would be no battles to fight.

And today I am saying it again.

Don't take your hurt and anger out into the world, and cause hurt and suffering to others.

Take the good you receive and share that instead.

※

Spirit says:

Each person on this earth lives a life separate from all others.

We think we know someone, and yet we don't ever really know their inner self. We only know ours. We know us.

Each life is also a separate world. The dreams are unique to that soul, to that person only. The experiences of that person are like no one else's. And the experiences, expectations, and disappointments of each person are unique.

And yet within the insular world of each person is a soul-need not to be alone. Existence means nothing without someone to share it.

A person alone would need a mirror to see what they look like. But when we belong to a family, and a tribe of like-minded friends, the mirror we need becomes those people. We see ourselves in the bloodline of family genetics. Same eyes. Same smiles. Same laughs. And we see ourselves within the circle of friends we've chosen, because we share the same joys for the same experiences.

. . .

It seems simple doesn't it? That we should all be able to get along. To agree. To live in harmony.

Yes, we should be able to do this.

But we don't.

We don't, because of that separate little world in which each soul exists. We don't because our experiences are not alike, so neither is our comprehension.

And so here we are. Living in our own separate little worlds, peering through the curtains we keep between us, afraid to step out, and be among strangers.

Fear keeps us trapped in a never-ending cycle of repetition.

And we hurt ourselves far worse by the choices we make, than from what anyone might do.

There are no easy answers to making any kind of change.

But the need for change exists.

The need for changing the way we treat each other is huge.

The question as to how many people on this earth are willing to do that is unknown, but that doesn't really matter.

All you need to know is that the change begins with you.

Sent with peace.
Sent with light.
Sent with love.

Spirit says:
Living in faith of something better, is what helps us persevere.

So there's the answer to every sad thought you've had today.

There's the answer to solving your anger.

There's the answer to indecision.

When you know something better is out there, it's easier to find it.

Believing that the end of your options to do better are where you are now, is living in defeat.

If you have problems, figure something out.

It's no one else's responsibility to fix it.

I once worked two jobs, besides all the jobs I had at home on the farm. I drove 5 miles to get to the first job that began at 7:30 a.m. and when it was over, I drove 30 more miles to get to the second one. I didn't get to leave for home until almost 10:00 p.m. and it was between 10:30 and 11:00 p.m. when I'd get home, with all that waited for me there.

I did this for almost two years.

Yes, I was tired. All the time.

But I did it for my family.

Ill health often prevents people from working. Sometimes we are the ones sick. Sometimes we're caring for someone else who's sick. But if you're healthy and able, and you're working as hard as you can, believing you will come out on the other side of debt and frustration, is what gets you through the hard times.

It's always about the choices you make, and the faith that you have in your own ability to do what has to be done to survive.

⁂

Yard Guy is outside mowing. Finally. It's rained so much for the past three weeks that there hasn't been a time when it would dry out enough for anyone to mow. And I'm only one in a long list of his customers. I certainly empathize for the day he has ahead of him.

. . .

When I was a little girl, Daddy cut our grass with a scythe because we didn't have a mower. When he finally got a push mower, I remember him and Mother being so excited about coming up in the world. I used to beg to use that mower, but I wasn't tall enough or strong enough to get it through the grass. After I got older, I did it a lot. We never did have a power mower.

When I lived out on the farm, before my divorce, we had a John Deere riding mower. I loved mowing. We had a huge yard, front and back, and the whole time I was mowing, I was thinking, and dreaming my stories, and that was long before I ever wrote that first book, even though the stories were always in my head.

It was before cell phones, and before we had a private line for a phone of our own in the house. There was just the party line that was more trouble than it was worth.

But riding around and around that yard, smelling the fresh cut grass, ignoring the garden out to the south that I knew was going to have to be hoed, or the vegetables I knew needed to be picked, was perfect. Getting on that riding mower was my "Calgon take me away" place to be.

Yes, I confess. I had a love affair with John Deere green.

So, thanks to Yard Guy, my yard will soon be all neat and tidy again.

Just like all the other yards in the neighborhood.

And my house, which looks pretty much like all the other houses in the neighborhood, will be in good standing with the HOA.

If I could just get my life in tune with my heart, I'd be good to go.

. . .

Sending you peace.
 Sending you light.
 Sending you love.

❧

I worked late, so I slept late.
 Spirit woke me with this message, but it is for all of YOU to read aloud to yourself, and to hear the words as if they are meant for you alone.
 It is your message of reassurance.

Spirit says:
 The world we live in now is in an upheaval.
 You feel as if it is your place to fix it before you can move forward.
 You want your old way back, but what some of you still don't understand is that for many, the old way was their constant hell.
 To fix what was broken, everything has to change.
 So Spirit sends this to humanity.
 Know this.
 Trust this these final words.

I don't know where I'm going.
 I just keep walking, walking, walking.
 I don't know my destination.
 But I trust my soul to lead me there.

❧

The day I planned did not happen.
 The milk was sour, so that changed breakfast.
 The cleaning lady was coming to clean and I was up early for

that, but I also promised to follow my daughter to take her son's truck in for repairs. She dropped it off at the dealer, and I brought her home, because he's with his dad and family on vacation.

I stopped on the way home to get milk, and when I got home, the cleaning lady had come and gone, but left me a note saying my vacuum cleaner quit.

My house smelled wonderful though, like Pinesol, so I marked one positive and one negative moment in my day, and headed to the office to Google vacuum repairs.

The nearest one was in the neighboring city, via eight-plus miles of city and interstate traffic. A city in which I only ever pass on the way to somewhere else. So I loaded up the dead Dyson, entered the address in Gertie Pearl Sala...(that's what I call my OnStar GPS) and off I went, only to drive up on the exit I needed to get off of I35, and find it's closed for repairs.

When I missed the exit, that threw Gertie Pearl into a tizzy, and she yelled at me for another quarter of a mile, until I finally got off and ended up driving into a neighborhood.

By then, Gertie's forgiven me and asking if I want to redirect, to which I replied, YES, and I received a new route that quickly got me there.

The repairman's name was Henry. Probably a little younger than me, but a character, which made me smile. By then I needed a laugh.. With the defunct Dyson dropped off (that's some fine alliteration, FYI), I finally headed home.

It was 12:30 by the time I walked in the door.

My daughter was here. She'd come to use my Jacuzzi on her aching back and legs. My house then smelled like Lavender Epsom Salts, and the Pinesol the cleaning lady used. But it didn't smell like food, so I called GrubHub. If I had the money, I'd buy stock in that place.

Food came. I ate. And I started to work, and then one last errand demanded my attention.

I just got home again. I'm tired. I'm not exactly in a mood, but let's just say, if I had chocolate I'd eat it.

However, I did put apples in to bake during the short time I was home today, so now my house smells like food, and as soon as I figure out what supper is going to be, I'm going back to work.

I can't call GrubHub again, or I'll have to apply for a job there to pay for it.

So today was what could have been a day of frustration.

But I chose to be happy.

And I chose to laugh about all of it, because I am in control of how I receive a change of plans.

Sending peace.

Sending light.

Sending love.

Spirit says: When the world does not comfort you in any way, find your own safe place to be. Accept that you cannot change anything but you.

When I know I have a differing opinion from most, you know what I do about that?

I keep it to myself. They didn't ask for it, and I don't feel the need to share it.

Everybody stays happy, and no one leaves mad.

When someone challenges my beliefs in hate or anger, it is the same thing as a physical blow to my spirit.

And when my spirit has been wounded, I feel it all over, and then I'm sad, and that carries on to others around me.

That's how negativity spreads.

It's an incurable virus.

A deadly virus.

And the cure begins with you.

Be the carrier of good will.
Be the healer of hurt feelings.
Be the purveyor of forgiveness.
Spread the light.
Spread the peace.
Spread the love.

Pest control guy was here early.

I had a massage mid-morning to ease some arthritic pains.

I am on a journey to Taking Care Of Me. Have you ever been there? It's worth the time and trouble, if you do.

A dichotomy of the value system within American people is valuing antique cars, the old Masters paintings, vintage jewelry, antique furniture, and looking upon elders as worthless and troublesome.

It's the perfect analogy for what's wrong in this world. We value things above people with wisdom and experience.

We don't want to hear about their life experiences because we're too wrapped up in our own.

But, oh the stories you are missing, and the lives they lived would put all of yours to shame.

They survived and thrived in ways you can't imagine.

Knowing you come from people who persevered and thrived is uplifting. It's like learning to tell directions so that you'll never be lost.

When you know that you're more than a wild night between two people who gave you life.

When you can see where your stubbornness comes from, and

why you have an innate sense of right from wrong, and why your hair is curly, or your nose turns up.

When you understand that you're here ONLY because they were here firs, then you begin to understand the vast circle of life, and your importance in it.

Leaving behind a good name and reputation, is worth more than all of the money and power a person could ever gain.

Leaving behind a legacy of surviving in spite of all odds, is worth everything to the generations to come.

It's something for them to aim for. Something for them to remember when the going gets tough.

Just to know that you come from people who figured it out, is a gift unto itself.

Live in kindness.

Live in gratitude.

Live in love.

༄

Spirit thanks you for the efforts you are making in your lives to do better - to be better, but reminds you it is a lifestyle, not a courtesy you offer to others when you feel like it.

You are also asked to remember that all souls are not on the same level of growth, and so the innate understanding they wish to achieve with each life they choose, may not be as advanced as another soul who's already moved past those levels of growth.

This is what often causes the separation between people of different races and beliefs. As a soul, they know everything about humanity and always live in a state of peace, love, and grace. But as a human they aren't allowed to remember. And it's the free will that they are given that moves their journey here on Earth.

So when that person doesn't know what's happening, and doesn't understand how to react, one of two things will happen.

They will either react in fear, which causes harm, or they will pause, and seek answers before reacting.

We are trying to birth a new way of being here.
 Birth is painful and messy and often frightening.
 But the new life that comes from birth is nothing short of a miracle. And right now, in this place, we are performing a miracle.
 Every day you put joy, peace, and kindness into the world, you are moving the birth forward. You are the inhale and the exhale, the bearing down and the push - you are part of the process of change - part of the Shift - part of creating a better place to live on an earth like this, but without the darkness of greed and evil, and Spirit thanks you.

Sending peace.
 Sending light.
 Sending love.

I have no troubles this morning because I did not accept them, and so off I went to the Farmer's Market to get some Porter peaches. They wound up being clings, not the freestones, but as a kid, all we ever grew were clings. No problems that I can see. I know how to peel fruit and cut it off the stone.
 As soon as my no-meat chicken strips are done, I'll have dinner, and then peaches for dessert. Yum.

Spirit says:
 A problem is like a rising creek. The longer you ignore it, the higher the water will rise, until you're at flood stage and cresting, and you've yet to even address that the problem is there.

That's procrastination.

My Little Mama loved that word. Procrastinate. A procrastinator. Someone who's good at procrastination.

In other words...putting things off.

Waiting for what they think is a more opportune time.

Not making a decision.

Not finishing a job.

Every year she'd have at least one student in her classroom who procrastinated. He/she would put off the assignment until the last minute, then be sitting at their desk, head down, writing furiously, eyeing the clock knowing that when the bell rang they had to hand it in, and shaking in their seat from the 'look' she was giving them.

I've been the recipient of that 'teacher look'.

I know the panic of not wanting to disappoint, and at the same time knowing it was my own fault because I'd put it off.

I'm still a little bit like that. I work better under pressure. When I don't have time to think about what I want to say or how I need to do something, it happens instinctively.

The words just come.

They're always there when I need them, which is a lot like how I think about God.

He's always there when I need Him, too.

Sent with peace.
Sent with light.
Sent with love.

A thunderstorm just blew through here...50 to 60 mph winds, blowing rain and hail.

Good morning, Oklahoma...

Most of it has passed and headed south, but now the house is cold. It was in the 80s yesterday, and today I turned on the heat before delivering Spirit's message.

Spirit says:
    Be gentle in all ways today.
    It is a day for contemplation.
    A day for being thankful.
    Move through the morning in quiet and kindness.
    Savor the hours of the afternoon as you reflect on all of the positive things in your life.
    Tonight before you sleep, don't forget to be thankful for all the ways you have been blessed.
    And so it is.

Sent with peace.
    Sent with light.
    Sent with love.

Spirit says:
Each time you face making a choice that will impact your life, you face two doors. They look alike, but there are two different worlds behind them, with paths that will take you in different directions.

And with each life choice you make as you age, you open yet another door, and yet another door, until you have gone through so many that you can no longer see the way you came.

This is why you don't dwell on the past. Why you don't use it as an excuse for why you're not where you want to be.

No one pushed you through a door, and you can't take back what's already been done.

You are where you are because of the doors only you have opened.

Spirit says, choose wisely.

Some doors stay shut for a reason.

Sometimes they are there to protect you.

To keep out what does not belong in your world.

It's not always about what you want to do.

But what you need to do.

What you must complete before you venture off onto another path.

There are always going to be doors in your life.

But you are the only key.

※

The shortest distance between two points is always a straight line.

But in life, taking shortcuts is what gets you into trouble.

If you skip the dips and curves in life, you miss the experiences, and the knowledge, you would have gained along the way.

It's like driving a car before you know what the controls are for.

Like stealing what you want because you're too lazy to work for it.

Or quitting school without an education.

Just because you are no longer traveling, doesn't mean you know where you are, or how you got there.

From the time you are born, your body is growing. And along the way, you are learning and excited about new ventures, and taking pride in your accomplishments.

Then somewhere along the way you became convinced that once you stopped growing, you became an adult.

You have decided you no longer needed guidance - that your education is complete. And now you're one of those struggling, because while you have the opportunity to view the same horizon as everyone else, you don't have the ability to get any closer.

Spirit wants you to know this is an analogy for how people view each other, as well.

Because we have all chosen certain paths, our lack of knowledge has automatically separated us from each other.

Because we don't know, then we can't understand.

And when we don't understand each other, the distance between us broadens, and deepens, until we no longer see each other as human beings.

We see enemies and strangers, and people to fear.

Because we chose a shortcut to understanding.

Because we decided not to learn about your ways.

Because we did not understand your appearance, we chose to fear you and to hate you.

And because we did not learn to discern a truth from a lie, we believe people who tell us what we want to hear, then become their minions...letting ourselves be herded into components of constant discord.

We took a shortcut and chose to disdain and discard.

We share the same earth.

We breathe the same air.

We are all pieces of God-light.

ALL OF US.

You who skipped this knowledge and understanding are the ones who don't get this.

It's not the responsibility of others to calm your anxieties, and change their ways to make you happy.

Being ignorant about humanity is on you.

Spirit says:
If you're out and about shopping today, take a moment to pick up some Kindness and Gratitude. You might be running low.

Don't forget you're always running out of Patience.

They have a deal on that. Just ask for it.

You'll find Peace located on the bottom shelf of your heart. It's a little dusty, but it never expires. Just clean it off and use it liberally.

Light is always on the top shelf, and shining like a beacon. You can't miss it.

And don't forget Love. You need an abundance to be able to share.

Sent with peace.
Sent with light.
Sent with love.

Spirit says:
"**When the world around you is so loud** that it's drowning out the sound of your own voice, then Whisper.

Everyone wants to know a secret,

And the softest voice can calm a crowd."

Make your journey today about care and kindness.

The world is so broken.

Humanity is suffering.

Be the compassionate witness.

Don't add to the pain that is already there.

Sent with peace.
Sent with light.

Sent with love.

Spirit says walk a quiet path today.
The world needs calm and peace, and it is up to us to make it so.

The energy of the world around us is in direct correlation to what we do and what we say.

We've been told this before. And we'll hear it again, and again, and again, until we finally get this right.

We didn't come here to destroy.

We came here to build. To grow. To love and encompass humanity as a whole.

We came to learn.

And we came to teach.

These were our purposes, but being human changed the course.

With the gift of free will, we lost focus.

And when you can't see clearly, then you don't see what's wrong.

Spirit isn't demanding anything of us.

These are reminders. Words of caution said with the same gentleness and love that a mother shows her child when she tells them to be careful.

Be careful today.

You are loved.

Sent with peace.
Sent with light.
Sent with love.

When I was a little girl, before I started school, Daddy called me Little Bit, and called my sister, Diane, Punkin.

I guess, because Father's Day has just passed, it prompted me to remember.

Sometimes the aches of things long past, are nothing more than fleeting memories – little shooting pains of the heart.

They're nothing to dwell on, and nothing to throw yourself into a funk about.

I think of those twinges as unprocessed grief.

That happens when someone else's death brings YOU responsibilities that weren't yours before, and you never take the time to really go through the stages of grief.

I have a lot of that, but then so do we all.

The trick is not to let it destroy you.

I'm working on that.

Spirit knows we're all struggling with different things.

There aren't any easy answers, and certainly no simple solutions.

Even on the days when I wish I was still Daddy's, Little Bit, and sitting on his lap beneath a shade tree listening to him talking to a neighbor who'd come to visit, I know that moment of joy that I saved in my heart, was for days when I can't remember joy.

I'm nobody's Little Bit anymore. I'm nobody's baby.

I didn't know my shy, quiet little self was destined to evolve into a stand-your-ground, warrior. That I would have to fight for everything, and everyone I loved, to keep them safe. That I would have to fight for my own right to be heard. And I didn't know that I would grow old alone.

What Spirit wants you to know is that, you're not alone in your struggles, and you don't need to feel defeated. You're not being punished for the hardships you're going through. It's just what being human is all about.

Sent with peace.
    Sent with light.
    Sent with love.

Spirit is all about empathy today. I haven't been able to read social media because everything is all about missing children, vicious crimes, and the continuing rage with each other about politics.

The ugly things that continue to happen in this country without justice being served, are all part of the dark side's plan. If we stay angry enough about people getting away with crimes, then they're free to wreak havoc about the world, unnoticed.

Try to understand what you're being fed is nothing but a slow poison. Don't always assume. What we see on the surface is never the whole truth. Be aware of the depths.

I continue to say prayers for my friends who are in health crisis, and I sent prayers to some friends who laid a loved one to rest today.

I sent love and healing to my two youngest granddaughters for the loss of their sweet dog, Macie. She was over 14 years old, and passed while they were all gone. It wasn't anyone's fault. It was just her time. But it doesn't make sad go away. That comes with time, and so I sent them love and prayers, too.

Spirit says if we want a better world, we have to be better in it.

Saying to no one in particular that "They need to do something" is like spitting in the wind. Useless words that come back to haunt us. It's not THEY. It's US. All of us. We have to be better to each other, or nothing is ever going to change.

I went to Farmer's Market this morning, and as my Daddy would say, I made a haul.

Fresh Porter peaches, handpicked blackberries, fresh baby beets, okra just begging to be fried, and huge homegrown tomatoes.

It was just like going to the garden when I was back on the farm, only better.

Happy day.

Spirit's message today is for people who are grieving.

There are two kinds of grief.

People who are living WITH grief.

And people who are living IN grief.

And yes, there is a difference.

People living with grief are the ones who have recently lost loved ones, and who are going through the stages of healing.

We have all lost people we love, and when that happens, we always go straight to OUR loss, instead of THEIR release. We think of the absence in our lives, but we don't think of the joy for them of going home.

Know that you are surrounded and loved by the generations of your ancestors, and your angels, and that you are being held within their energy to help you heal.

The people who are living IN grief are the ones who don't know how to let go. Years have passed since the death, and they've lost their way to the point that they're not living out their OWN lives anymore.

They have immersed themselves into being the victims of an absence.

They identify as the orphan, the widow, the person who lost a child, lost a wife, etc.

They greet each day in sadness. They don't see the rest of their family as valid. They focus only on who's no longer there.

And because they are so locked into grief, they create this image in their minds of their loved one in spirit, wandering sad and lost, when in reality, that image is them.

Spirit wants you to know that YOUR inability to let go, saddens the spirits of your loved ones who have long since crossed over. They want you to let go. They want you to move on, and to thrive, and to laugh again. When you put your whole life in limbo, you have, in essence, died with them, because you stopped living, too.

It is my personal belief that it is not only my honor, but also my duty, to live my best life for my loved ones who have passed.

We, who are left behind, are here for a reason, and it has nothing to do with living with the dead.

Climb out of that hole and be you again.

That's not forgetting your loved ones are gone.

It's honoring that they lived.

Sent with peace.
Sent with light.
Sent with love.

&

Spirit wants to remind you that the door into a kinder, gentler way of existing is always open, but you have to be in a place of peace within humanity to get in.

. . .

Prejudice does not exist there, and hate is not a word.

The color of someone's skin means nothing in that place.

There, Love is a verb in action, and you feel it without and within.

Joy is enveloped within the air you breathe.

Kindness is a given, and gratitude is a way of living.

There is no map to getting there.

The path and the key are within you, holding space, waiting for your understanding to reach that level of acceptance.

Spirit also wants you to know that it's okay if you're not ready yet. It only means you have more spiritual growth to attain.

If you aren't yet able to see past the dark ones lies, then that is your path in this lifetime.

If you still make excuses for injustice, then you are on a different level of learning.

It doesn't make you wrong. It just means you are a younger soul with much to learn.

There is a hint of a gentle reminder to those souls, that judging others is not for them.

That is left to the Great I Am, to God, to their Creator.

There is also a gentle reminder to those who advocate violence, to study the history of the Earth they now inhabit, so that they might be reminded that it has never, in the existence of the Universe, created a safe place to be.

Sent with peace.
  Sent with light.
  Sent with love.

Spirit says, in all things - Be prudent. Be careful. Be aware.

The fear mongers who work with the dark side are at work daily keeping the world in turmoil. The horrific crimes - the missing children - casting blame, throwing shade, inciting racial and religious persecution - It's all part of their plan.

While you have been incited by fear, rage, and grief, the dark ones grow stronger. When you let yourself be led down those paths, you are succumbing to their plans.

When you believe every outrageous thing you read without researching for facts, you are falling right into their hands.

When something seems too outrageous to be true, and you pass it on as gossip, anyway, then you are participating in their lies.

You have become their minions to stirring up trouble.

If that suits your needs and your beliefs, then so it is.

You are where you are, and you're doing what you're doing with the free will God gave you.

However, I would suggest you consider that God expected more of you than this.

This is a crucial time for humanity.

Stand in a place of love.

Stand in God-light.

Stand in a place of peace.

Sent with peace.

Sent with light.

Sent with love.

&.

When I was a little girl, Mother was always repeating herself to me..."Sherry, did you hear me? Were you listening to me?"

Most of the time I was, but quite often in my life, and sometimes even now, my body is in one place, but my thoughts are in another.

. . .

When we were a little older, Mother would send Diane and me to the garden to pick the green beans, or pull some radishes and onions for dinner, or send us to pick a few yellow squash for her to fry up.

I was focused on the task right up to the point when I was down on all fours between the rows, and all of a sudden I was somewhere else living out the fantasy in my head. And fifteen minutes later Mother was yelling at me out the kitchen window..."Sharon Kay...are you working?" My head would come up from between the rows and I'd yell back...."I am now!"

Bobby was always teaching me to be aware, but I didn't know it then. It's only now as I think back to him telling me - "Baby, just pay attention and you'll see it. Pay attention and you'll find it. Pay attention and you will understand."

And he was right. I am aware of everything. The signs are all around of Spirit showing us - guiding us - warning us. All you have to do is pay attention.

Like me. This morning.

In nice weather, I go barefoot in the house, and barefoot outside my house, all the time. And this morning I glanced out the front window as I started to go get the newspaper, and then stopped.

In my head, I heard Spirit saying "Put on shoes. It will cut your feet."

I almost ignored it. And then I remembered Bobby saying, "Pay attention, baby," and so I put on shoes and went out. I walked down the driveway, and when I bent over to get the paper, I began seeing tiny bits of something white all over the concrete. I picked the first one up and it was curved, and hard and sharp. It would have gone straight into my food. And then I begin looking and there were dozens of little shards of broken PVC pipe. I don't know where it came from, or why it was in my driveway, but my feet would have been shredded if I'd walked on that.

I brought the paper back inside, then went back out with a broom and a dustpan and swept up every little piece.

I wasn't hurt because I paid attention to the voice.

All of us have this ability. You just have to learn to be quiet within yourself to hear. And then you trust. It's your instinct for survival - your self-preservation. Whatever you want to call it, it's still the guiding Spirit within you, trying to keep you safe.

Sent with peace.
Sent with light.
Sent with love.

Spirit says:
God doesn't make mistakes.
Be you.
Be the example of beauty within.
Clean body, clean hair, clean clothes, and a happy disposition is all it takes.
Dress to please yourself.
Be who you are in the world, not who other people want you to be.
When you let other people's opinions be the guiding force throughout your life, you are giving away your power.
There is no such thing as a Department of Public Opinion.
The Fashion Police aren't real. They're just a bunch of unhappy people who make fun of others because they don't like who THEY are.
Just because your friends are laughing at someone else's misfortune doesn't mean you have to laugh, too.

Be the empathetic witness.

Be the voice of reason.
Be the one who speaks up for injustice.
Be the one who says Stop.
Be the one who says No.
Sent with peace.
Sent with light.
Sent with love.

※

When I was a little girl, having a birthday was a big deal. Mother would make me a cake, and put one candle in the middle of it so I could make a wish.

I can't remember even one wish from those days, but I can promise you they had nothing to do with where my life has taken me.

I would never have dreamed I'd become a writer, or that technology would evolve to the point that I could communicate daily with so many wonderful people.

My life was a simple one. What we had was enough. I didn't ask for more than what I already had. It just wasn't how life worked for us back then, and looking back, I know now it was the family into which I was born, that was my blessing. Receiving gifts is fun, but it's the givers who mean the most to me.

Treasure the moments of joy and laughter within your life.
Be grateful for the people in it.
Take nothing for granted.
Life is precious, but the time that we are given here is unknown.
Don't part company in anger with someone you love.
Be the peacemaker.
Be the light for your family.

Be the example of what it means to love.
Today, the third of July, is my birthday.
Another year of life is behind me.
And that is the gift.

Sent with peace.
    Sent with light.
    Sent with love.

※

When I was little, Fourth of July meant going to the carnival in town. But we never went until evening, because farmers don't take off in the middle of the day to go play.

As a kid, the carnival rides were like magic. All the lights, the hurdy-gurdy sounding music coming from the merry-go-round, and the big decision of which horse to ride. I always chose a black one with its head thrown back. You know, the one that looked like it was about to buck off the rider.

Yeah, that one. I was a real daredevil back then.

I wanted to ride the rides, but I also had motion sickness, so by the time we'd spent our ride money, I was usually staggering, and a bit sick.

The carnival always set up across the road from the city park, and when the sun began moving toward the western horizon, people started showing up in the park with quilts and picnic baskets. They'd spread their quilts, and take the food out of the baskets, and the families would eat supper on the ground, while waiting for it to get dark, which was when the fireworks would begin.

But since I'd made myself sick on the rides, the idea of food never set quite right with me, so I picked at what was there, and then Diane and I would run like little puppies turned loose from a pen, shrieking and chasing each other around the park with all of the other kids who where there.

Until it began to get dark.

That's when we knew it was time to get back to 'our quilt', and so we'd race back through the grass, now getting damp from the falling dew, and drop down in the middle of Mother and Daddy's laps, puffing and red-faced, and begging for a drink.

Mother always told us we smelled like sweaty puppies.

Daddy told us we just smelled like fun.

Sometimes my Grand and Grampy would be sitting there on the quilt when we came back, and sometimes it would be my Grandpa and Grandma Smith. I remember one time Grandpa Smith gave me a dollar, because it was my birthday the day before, and I spent the whole thing at a side show trying to win a teddy bear. I got a pinwheel instead. Life lesson learned.

What you want and what you get can be two different things.

The signal that fireworks were beginning, was always one big boom. I used to think it was a cannon, but since there wasn't a cannon in town, it was likely just a big firecracker. And then the sky lit up in a way that always felt like magic. Roman candles...huge explosions of color, and what looked like stars falling down from heaven.

Diane and I would lie flat on our backs to watch. Sometimes I'd lay my head in my Grand's lap, or lean against Mother's shoulder.

Once a year, it was a night of magic.

When we packed up to leave, sometimes Mother would put the quilt in the back of our old pickup and Diane and I would ride home back there, looking up at the stars. We always fell asleep on the way home.

Daddy carried us in the house, and Mother would put us to bed.

That seems like another life - in another world.

A world too far away to visit anymore.

The memories are still with me, but I'm the only one left in my family from that time.

Maybe that's why it's so hard to get back there now.

I can't say, 'remember when', because there's no one left to remember with me.

So, this post is a 'remember when' from me to you.

❦

Sometimes I feel like Spirit's messages are an echo, that I've said all that needs to be said, and the messages are landing on deaf ears, and fading fast.

The situation in this country is apparent.

You either are fine with it, or you're not.

You argue or you don't.

You rage at other people who don't agree. Every. Day.

And still haven't figured out they don't care what you think, because their agenda is not yours.

Social Media is not the platform for change.

That comes with bombarding the people in power with your anger or your approval. Not your neighbor. Not your friend.

Spirit is talking to me, and I'm sharing the words, and half of you hear, and half of you don't, and that's okay with me. I KNOW how this world works. I don't expect blanket approval because we're not all alike.

Spirit keeps telling me to remind you all....WE'RE NOT SUPPOSED TO BE ALIKE.

But as with all things human, the need to be heard, often overrules common sense, and any kind of consideration for humanity.

What you might not understand, or even care about, is that it's hard for me to see the blindness in people, because I know where I came from, and I know where I will go when I die, and I know how this world works. And all of this discord makes me sad - so sad.

I have been coming back to this planet for thousands and thousands of years - in many other lifetimes. And every trip has been about trying to help people into living in a higher ascension, and I'm never coming back here again, because I don't want to.

My patience with hate is used up.

My empathy for people who are hurting others in an effort to live life their way is used up.

I'm done with selfish.

I'm over it.

My focus at the end of this life is on people who want to change.

The others don't need the messages. They aren't ready to hear them.

I wish to God I had the power to heal both emotional and physical pain, but I don't. In this lifetime, I'm just a messenger.

Sent with peace.
   Sent with light.
   Sent with love.

※

Spirit asks these questions of you.
   If you had nothing to fight about, what would you do?
   Do you know how to go through a day in a calm and peaceful manner?
   Are you aware there are places in the world where discord does not exist?
   Could you go an entire day without complaining?
   Must there always be someone who displeases you?
   Do you not know how to just walk away without engaging in battle?
   Why does nothing ever satisfy you?

What is it that drives you to constant disapproval?

Why can't you leave well enough alone?

Why do you always see what's wrong and never look for what is right?

Spirit isn't accusing. Spirit asks.

Do you see yourself here?

It's not our place to judge each other, but it is imperative that we see the truth in ourselves.

Sent with peace.

Sent with light.

Sent with love.

❧

Day before yesterday I found a perfect goose feather in the grass, sticking up like a flag on a pole, just waiting for me.

Finding feathers are signs from your angels that they are with you, and know that you are in need of comfort.

Yesterday on the way home from church I stopped at a store. I was thinking about Bobby when I got out, and when I came out there was a penny near the door of my car. He's the master of the penny trails, and I knew it was there because I'd been thinking of him, and he wanted me to know he knew it.

Angels.

Your loved ones.

The messages are all around you.

Like Bobby always told me, "Just pay attention, baby."

The signs are there.

You're not alone.

And you are loved.

. . .

Sent with peace.
>Sent with light.
>Sent with love.

❧

Spirit has one message this morning.
The person you were, does not matter as much as the person you are.
The one you have become.
Yes, one shapes the other to a degree, but there is always opportunity to shift focus, and step onto a new path.
If the one you are on continues to take you in the wrong direction, then you might want to consider the choices you are making.
Everything in life is a ripple effect of the first step, the first choice, the first words uttered in a new day.
Be aware.
Be certain this is the life you want, and the path you need to take to get to it.

Sent with peace.
>Sent with light.
>Sent with love.

❧

The louder the world gets, the quieter I become.
I hear the noise.
But I refuse to live within chaos, and if I have to remove myself to find the quiet places, then I will.

Spirit says:
Our souls did not come from a place of discord, and living

within a human body, and adapting to all of the earthly shortcomings is hard enough.

Chaos and discord can either make us angry, or make us afraid.

That is not how being human was meant to be. But it is what we have become because of the free will we were given when we came.

People who feel emotionally attacked, think they are feeling sadness and fear, but what they're actually doing is recognizing and rejecting that way of life.

Those souls came with purpose, but have found themselves in a climate of such unrest that they cannot focus on their path, and spend their time here on earth in disarray and confusion.

Some become hermits.

Some become cold and angry, rejecting any measure of friendship, or companionship, because they've been betrayed one too many times.

Some lose their sanity and wander the streets, too broken by the ugliness of this world, and simply waiting for their time to go home.

It is upon us to winnow the chaff from the wheat.

To remove the people from our own lives who do not fit into our place of peace. The people who've already hurt you, or frightened you, the ones who've proven they can't be trusted.

And when the world gets too loud, then you walk away to your quiet place, and you find a way to reset your course, without anyone else's input. Without following someone else's rules for life. Or, you can stay where you are, let everything and everyone control your life, and sink your own ship.

It's all on you to decide.

. . .

Sent with peace.
    Sent with light.
    Sent with love.

Spirit sends this message to you today.
    It is within your power to change the energy within you, and around you, by how you act, and how you receive.
    Find the way to be in harmony, and the solace you bring to the world will be immeasurable.
    It will also give balance to your life, and to the decisions that you make.
    Nothing lasts forever, so accept that you will always be evolving.

For some, life is exactly how they want it. They are living a life that feels good, and they are living in prosperity and abundance.
    But there are others with lives that are cycling. They have been moved out - some dumped out most abruptly - from the calm within which they'd become accustomed.
    They are in free-fall and it's scary and upsetting, and it feels like nothing is ever going to be okay again.

But it will.
    Like water, life always finds its own level.
    And when it does - when the flood of emotions in free-fall have passed, and they are able to see bits and pieces of what lies ahead, they will settle, and put down new roots, and find a new way to be.
    Change can be good, and change can be sad - so sad.
    But as long as you still draw breath, your job is to be as good a person within this place that you are in, as you know how to be.

That is what it means to be living a life.

Sent with peace.
    Sent with light.
    Sent with love.

☙

Spirit's message today is...."Do the right thing first."

As we go through our lives, we see how society works, and how laws and jobs, and people living out their lives are evolving.

We know what we're supposed to do to exist.

We know what's supposed to happen, but other people's free will, and the choices they make often impact us, as well.

That's why it's so important to live a life doing no harm.

It's enough that your own choices sometimes put your life in turmoil, but when your choices impact and harm others, it becomes its own disaster.

At that point, saying 'I'm sorry,' is rarely enough.

You've hurt too many others with your selfishness.

Your thoughtlessness toward others has caused infinite ripples through countless other lives, and all because you didn't think before you spoke, or think of the consequences of your own actions.

I had a stalker once. The damage she did to my cars, to the horses, to my property, to my life, were indescribable. All she could focus on was hurting me. And then I caught her. I had evidence. And I got a restraining order against her. And so she started sneaking around, doing more, causing more and more trouble, until we all wound up in court, and there's me, and there's Bobby, and I'm on the stand, with my evidence. And there she is, sitting in court with her mother and her family, thinking she was going to see the both of us being destroyed because she hated me that much for absolutely nothing I did. Just because of who I was.

And then she wound up on the stand, and everything she'd been doing to me was revealed, and she couldn't deny it, and she couldn't hide in the shadows anymore, and her whole family witnessed it, and her shame.

Her need to destroy me spilled over into her world, into her family who had no idea of what she'd been doing, and they sat there in silence, stunned, hearing her admit to what she'd done.

I never knew how her world played out, and didn't care.

Bobby died not long afterward, and I was done with that place, and those people. Those people who turned a blind eye to truth, and reveled in seeing someone else's suffering.

I have been a victim of other people's random choices to hurt and harm. I have been the collateral damage.

But I am also the survivor.

I didn't cause the trouble, but I ended it.

Because I did the right things first.

Sent with peace.
   Sent with light.
   Sent with love.

ঌ

A story I just read in the news reminded me of something that happened between me and my grandson, who we call Scout. It happened when he was barely 3 years old - and today I felt Spirit nudge...'tell them'.

It will be telling a story that, for fifteen years, has mostly been between me and family, and a few close friends.

But Spirit said tell them, and I cannot ignore the request.

. . .

Before I was divorced, I used to drive the hour and a half from the farm up to the city where my daughter and her family lived, at least three times a month - more often if she needed me.

On this day, I was going up just for a visit, and to take back some clothes I'd altered for Scout, because even at 3 years old, he was so tall for his age.

So I'd been there from around 10:00 in the morning to mid-afternoon, and I was thinking about getting ready to leave.

But before I left town, it was always our thing to take Scout and my daughter for ice cream. Only this particular summer day, I think she was in the middle of canning something and was too busy to go, so I loaded my big three-year old in the front seat, because he was already tall enough to ride up front without a booster seat, then buckled him in, and off we went.

As we're driving, he said, "Gwammy, can we dwive with the window down. I like the wind."

I hate heat, but I loved my grandson, and I said, "Absolutely, we can," and I rolled down his window, and lowered mine a bit, and we're off. And now the wind is blowing those red curls on his head, and he's looking out the window, and looking up at the clear blue sky, dotted with wisps of white clouds. And I start noticing how intently he is inspecting it.

And then he says. "Gwammy, isn't dis a pwetty day?"

I smiled, and I said, "Yes, baby, it sure is."

Then he turned that 3-year-old baby face toward me, and with the most angelic smile on his face, he said, "It's just like the day Jesus died."

For a couple of seconds, I forgot to breathe. I was stunned by what had just come out of his mouth. Only three years from heaven, and he still remembered all that he'd known before.

Finally, I gathered myself and managed a response. "Really?"

He nodded. "It was pwetty just like this...before the storm."

There was nothing to say. I just reached over, and patted his little hand, knowing in that moment how old his soul, and what a gift our family had been given by his birth.

I wondered then, as I do now, what he will do. What he'll become.

But what I do know for sure is that he's been on his path since the day he was born, and the choices he's made have rarely been wrong. He has never once lied to any of us. Not even a fib when he was little. And his heart is just as big as he is now.

I think the reason Spirit wanted this told is for people not to see children as little people who are to be molded into replicas of someone else. And to realize that sometimes the children born into a family are older souls than the people who will raise them.

That maybe they came here to be the examples of how we're supposed to be. That when they show empathy and kindness to people their parents might not approve of, that it's the parents who need the lessons in how to behave, and not the children.

Anyway, I have told you now, what has been a special thing within our family. Scout has no memory of this anymore. And that's how it works here on earth. But I remember. I already know this about him. And now so do you.

So look at the little ones in your lives...and at the babies who are just now being born.

Think before you start teaching them how to look, and who to like, and what to think.

Think hard before you decide you need to turn them into people with prejudice and hate.

They come so pure.

And then we contaminate them and the world into which they've been born, and all that purpose they knew, and their knowledge of who they were, and where they've been in lifetimes before, is buried beneath what being human on this earth currently means.

. . .

I have dreams of a day when Earth will be a place when everyone lives with that wisdom, and innocence, and that kind of pure honesty and truth.

Sent with peace.
   Sent with light.
   Sent with love.

Spirit says:
Surround yourself with things that are beautiful to you...flowers, pictures, an old dish from your grandmother's cupboard as the centerpiece for your dining room table, a fresh baked cake...the people you love....it goes on and on.

Humans need creature comforts to feel safe, and to be happy in this world, like decent places to live, food to eat, clothes to wear, and a job that provides all this for them.

But the soul requires the intangibles to be comfortably centered in this human existence.

Intangibles like joy, peace, kindness, love, and the sight of beautiful things that are special to only you. Even if it is nothing more than a clean and shiny floor, then that is enough.

If you are feeling the burden of life right now, change your surroundings in some way. Move furniture. Put flowers in a vase. Hang a picture.

And if it's outside, put up a bird bath or a bird feeder, and enjoy the show, because there will be one.

Adding beauty into your surroundings is not only pleasing to the eye, but healing to your soul.

Turn off the television.
Read a book.
Go for a walk.
Go to lunch with a friend.
Don't take pictures of your food.
Take pictures of you and your friend.
Make memories.
The days will come when those are all you will have left of them.

Sent with peace.
    Sent with light.
    Sent with love.

I thought I was going to bed and then this happened. So I'm delivering it now because I am a messenger.

Spirit wants to remind you:
    God didn't make the United States of America.
    God made Earth.
    Earth is a part of The Universe.
    It is not the beginning, nor is it the end of anything.
    It is a place that the humans we are inhabit.
    He loves all of us because we are all His children.
    Not just the chosen few you think you are.
    Stop asking God to fix the mess you're in.
    Humans created the mess.
    It's not God's mess to fix.

You can't pray your way out of a dying Earth.
    You destroyed it with chemicals and waste and greed.

You want peace, but at your price - not for humanity, but so that life is how you want to live it.

You had your chance to rise above what's happening, and you decided you're rather fight some more...

At least another two or three thousand years.

You want things better, then do better.

You want peace, then stop fighting.

You want love, then stop hating on others.

You want, want, want.

But you aren't willing to give.

You don't admire, you covet.

If you don't say thank you for what you have and are given, you won't have anything left for which to be thankful.

That which is given to you can also be taken away.

Your birthright has nothing to do with money.

You are a child of God.

Act like one.

༄

It is so hot and so dry here, so I watered the back yard yesterday, and up into the night until I went to bed.

Oh...the joy it caused.

Birds, birds, birds...in the trees, on the fence, in the grass, and every time I came out to move the sprinkler, they just sang and sang.

I made them happy...and their songs made me happy, and such is the circle of life.

We give to each other.

We do for each other.

And when we do, love for each other can only grow.

Abundance for what matters most comes from within us.

When you do no harm, you cause no harm.

And the energy of such a small thing always sends a ripple effect throughout the Universe.

Think of it like this...

When one porch light comes on at night, that house stands out in the darkness. But if all the lights come on in one big city all at once, it can be seen from space, and so it goes.

Your kindness is a light, both without and within. But as a whole, we glow.

Sent with peace.

Sent with light.

Sent with love.

Spirit says:

Stop talking so much, and listen more.

I'm not sure what this will mean to you personally, but there it is.

Maybe it means you are ignoring the obvious because a lie suits your beliefs more than a truth...and living within a lie is not a healthy way to be.

Maybe it means you aren't focusing on what's really important.

Do you tune your family out when they are trying to talk to you because you're too focused on social media...or what's on your phone instead of what's before you?

Maybe Spirit is telling you that your children are in crisis, and you're not listening closely enough to what they're 'not' saying.

Maybe it means you are afraid to stop talking, for fear of the answers you might receive. Maybe you think if you say something often enough it will be a fact.

I don't know...and it's not my business to know.

I am the messenger, and you are the recipient, so it is yours to decipher or ignore.

. . .

Just be at peace with the message, regardless.

It isn't a warning. It is simply a message.

Like your mother when you were little telling you why it's important to look both ways before crossing a street.

You listened then and learned, and you're still alive because you learned.

So now...Spirit gives you another message.

And if you follow the suggestion, a whole new way of looking at life could be opened to you.

Sent with peace.
    Sent with light.
    Sent with love.

❧

I'm going to see Lion King today.

It's a remake, but then so am I, because I've been this way before.

I'm going just to get out of the house.

Normally, I wouldn't want to see it again, because I've seen the original movie somewhere around a hundred times...and I know how it ends.

It first came out in 1994, and I took my first granddaughter to see it when she was only 3 years old. It was the first movie she'd ever been to, and it was quite a trip for both of us.

She was in awe of the big screen, but after it began, she crawled up in my lap to watch it, because there was so much growling and roaring, and Scar was mean. So she just pulled her blankie up a little closer under her chin, and leaned against me. I took that as my cue to hold her tighter, and so we watched it together. It was the quietest I ever knew her to be when she was awake.

After that, I got the DVD of Lion King, and then I was blessed with two more granddaughters, thus came the 'watching the movie' at least a hundred times, because there was much lap sitting, and hugging, and blankies pulled up beneath more little baby chins.

So I guess today is just me wanting to be with family again, and Scout volunteered to take my daughter and me.

Granted...Scout, who at the moment, is 6'4", does not need a lap to sit in. And there will be no need for blankies. But there will be popcorn and cold drinks, and much roaring and stampeding, and Scar will still be mean, and that's okay, because we all understand that I already know how this ends.

⁂

I long ago accepted the quiet warrior that I am.

But, I also accept the southern part of my upbringing with the same joy I get when someone adds another scoop of taters and gravy to my plate.

My life was shaped by the things that happened to me, and how I survived them, but my taste buds grew to adulthood on southern food.

My potatoes are your pasta.

My biscuits and gravy are your bread and butter.

My fried okra is your eggplant Parmesan.

My beans and cornbread is your Mulligan stew.

My coconut cream pie is your Cannoli.

My cornbread dressing is your oyster dressing.

Whatever you love is what you love, whether it's the slow drawl in a southern voice, or the clipped accent of a northerner.

Being different is what makes us special.

Being me is what makes me comfortable.

And being you is what you do best.

We could be US together.

Not US apart.

But we'd have to stop arguing about who was wrong, and who was right.

Yeah...we'd have to do that first.

Sent with peace.
Sent with light.
Sent with love.

Spirit says:
Remember.
Remember your soul did not always exist in this place.

Remember that you are here for a time, but this is not your forever home.

Remember that you are so loved, and that your soul family is always with you. Your guardian angels are always with you, and the great I AM from which you came is always and forever with you.

You are never really lost.

Remember that your journey here was not a vacation.

That you came with purpose.

If you can't remember that purpose, then live the best life you can without causing another soul to hurt, and you will have done enough.

Spirit also wants you to remember that you did not come here to conquer, but to create.

War is for the dark ones.

Love and harmony comes with the light.

You fuss about people not getting along, but the simple fact that you are complaining about it is part of the problem.

My Little Mama used to get upset about everything, as her dementia worsened.

Nothing made her happy except for chocolate.

I could redirect her displeasure or sadness in a heartbeat, with a hug and a Hershey kiss. And that worked all the way up to the day she forgot what chocolate was, and would no longer put it in her mouth.

So think about what the people around you are fussing about, and if it's nothing but different points of view, and displeasure with the world around them, then maybe all they need is a hug, and a piece of chocolate.

Think about it.

Sometimes, all you need is to know someone is listening.

Sometimes, what you need to remember is that you walk with angels...and you are loved.

Sent with peace.
    Sent with light.
    Sent with love.

        ❧

Here I am, up at 6:00 a.m. when I don't have to be, and all because of a dream, and Spirit's insistence I write it down before I forget the details because it is a message. Le sigh! And my pillow was so comfy.

Anyway.

In the dream I went home to my People - to the Native world of the past.

I am only a visitor in this dream. I do not participate. I watch a medicine man healing people of different ailments.

One man comes to him with an ache in his side and the medicine man looks, and feels, and then rubs something on the man's side, and a few seconds later pulls out the broken tip of an arrowhead from an old wound. The wound had healed, but left something behind from the war he'd been in.

The next person to come, complained of a stomach ache. and again, the medicine man went through the same process, and then somehow his fingers just slipped into the man's belly without cutting skin, or making anything bleed, and pulled out a small rock. He tells the man that it was in a stew he ha eaten, and that he should chew before he swallows.

And so it went. One person after another with things that were hurting them, that had been caused by their own actions.

And then a young boy with braids hanging almost to his waist, brings in a small tortoise. The little boy dark eyes are teary, and fear-filled. He loves his little pet, and thinks it is dying.

The medicine man sees that the little tortoise seems to be having what looks like a seizure. It's feet are stiff and trembling, and it's neck and head are out and shaking. Instead of retreating in its shell, it appears as if it wants to escape.

The medicine man turns the little tortoise over and sees no obvious injuries anywhere, and then he looks deep into its eyes, and sees terror. Sheer terror.

And then he looks closer within the shell, gasps, then quickly holds the tortoise over smoldering sage and sweet grass, letting the smoke completely engulf the little tortoise. Then he puts the tortoise down on its belly. As soon as he does that, a large spider comes crawling out of its shell. Immediately, the little tortoise quits trembling, and quickly retreats into its shell. The little boy is elated and leaves with his pet.

In those dreams, when I am but a watcher, the people never see me, unless they are very spiritual, or if there is a message. And in this dream, the medicine man looked up at me and said. "There is a spider in the shell."

Thus, the reason I was up at 6:00 a.m. - researching what turtles and spiders represent within the People, and this is what I found.

I'm still a bit rattled by the message, because it is a powerful one for me --- for all of us.

In Native American lore, a turtle is the symbol of a peace-maker, and of the sacred feminine.

And Grandmother Spider spins the web of time and knows all aspects of the future and the past.

Spirit is saying that, Grandmother Spider's appearance signifies the change, and a new way of peace is coming, bringing the rise of the sacred feminine.

The turtle - the little peacemaker - was afraid of the change, but once it understood its purpose, the spider left. The message had been delivered.

And the Medicine Man looking directly at me meant it was my job to take the message out of the Spirit world, and give it to you.

And so it is.

Sent with peace.
  Sent with light.
  Sent with love.

𝕱

The moment my feet hit the floor this morning, Spirit was in my head...tell them...tell them.

And I replied..."Just let me get this load of laundry started first, please!"

So the load is washing, I haven't had breakfast, but I'm here...passing on the message.

. . .

Spirit says remember we all come with different purposes, but with the same edict - with the same rule. "Do unto others, as you would have them do unto you."

So...okay...so most of us know that...but Spirit's message is what I would call "a reminder."

Good or bad, you do "unto others" all the time. But that which you do to others WILL BE done unto you. Eventually. Through karma. From the Universe. From your own manifestations of creating revenge, and through your own anger.

If your actions are done through envy, greed, revenge, or a false sense of duty to tell others how to live their lives - then every negative bit of energy you are creating to hurt someone else, WILL come back on you.

Every time someone shouts, "THIS is God's country," and uses it as a means of setting themselves apart as better or special, or falsely believing God is only where certain people gather - what only certain people believe - they have chosen to ignore the obvious truth. They think small. And they are living in a little bubble of misinformation and belief.

Look up. THAT is God's country...His Universe.

He created all of us, and all of that.

HE IS CREATION. HE IS LIFE. HE IS LOVE.

Spirit says: You cannot have only half a truth to suit your purposes. How YOU treat people, and how you ACT towards them, and what your SAY about them, is what is coming to you.

So: Message delivered.

How you receive it is your business.

What you choose to receive is from your own free will.

There is no need to justify anything you do or say to me.

You go talk to God about that.

I'm just the messenger, who has laundry to tend.

Sent with peace.
    Sent with light.

Sent with love.

※

Going to get my teeth cleaned this morning, but I want to be in bed.

I am so tired.

I wake up that way.

I go through my day that way.

I am emotionally sick at heart, and today I am done with people.

I'll get past this feeling. I always do.

But today I'm just going to mind my own business, and quietly pray for the families who are burying their dead.

They don't want to hear our opinions of who was responsible for their loved ones' murders. They're trying to notify family, and come up with the money to bury them.

Children have been orphaned.

Families decimated.

And total strangers are bandying the incident around like it's a multiple choice question on a test. One of those 'which answer best fits the scenario' questions.

You don't have to know who died to show compassion.

It's the same thing as pulling over onto the shoulder of the road, and stopping for a passing funeral procession.

Whether you admit it or not.

Whether you even know it or not.

Our country is at war and the enemy is within.

We are not safe.

Two years ago, I was saying love one another and it would change the world.

But, that wasn't the choice that was made, and here we are.

I'm writing this and crying because I am so sad for all of us.

. . .

Spirit is but a witness to this.

God won't fix this because He didn't break it.

We did. Through the free will we were promised when we came.

And the only way it's going to change is with us, only we can't agree on anything. And no one wants to concede. Everyone wants life done their way.

So have at it.

Wave your flags.

Brandish your guns.

Bury your dead.

And go fight your wars.

I want nothing to do with any of it, or any of you.

I do not belong to the tribe of prejudice and hate.

Another day to gather my thoughts into a semblance of peace of gratitude for what is pleasing to my heart.

I have shut out those who perpetuate my sadness.

Blocked those who's purposes and thoughts are poison to me.

I am not saying any of those people are wrong.

I am saying they are wrong for me.

My life.

My path.

My beliefs are holy to me.

No one else gets to inject my space with discord because it is my space.

They are free to run wild on their own.

Spirit says:

"Bring order to where you live and what you do, and your inner peace will come.

If chaos abounds around you, then you have let it in.

You have the power to set your own boundaries, but if you have chosen to let others opinions and suggestions become your way of life, then you have given away your power to them.

Yes, you might agree with them, and then that is fine.

But if you were wavering between two things, and did not make your own decisions, then you gave away your free will to someone else, and you now have no right to complain of the end results.

Sent with Peace.
Sent with Light.
Sent with love.

Spirit says:

The approach to a good life is not to plan it, but to just live it.

Then, when something you 'planned' didn't work out, there is no disappointment to face. No failure to feel.

It's simply a matter of taking a deep breath, and looking up to see where you are.

There are always exits to a situation.

You don't have to like them.

But you do have to remember and accept that your free will and your choices are what got you there, and they will be what gets you out.

Exchanging energy.
Giving and accepting.
Honoring and learning.
And so it is.

Sent with peace.
   Sent with light.
   Sent with love.

It's finally raining. Not a downpour, just a soft, gentle rain. I have never been so grateful for the sound of rain coming through the downspout of a gutter.

The birdseed in the feeder got wet. I just dumped it out before it sprouted inside the feeder, which has happened before. It won't hurt the bigger birds feelings to have everything down on the ground below it, and it will make red squirrel's day because the sunflower seeds in it will be easy to get to.

Yes, I feed the rabbit beneath my garden shed. And the squirrel that runs across the top of my fence. And the tiny mouse I sometimes see in the flowerbeds, and the birds...especially the doves. Bobby sends me those.

So, here's the deal people.

Spirit knows my soul is sad. Spirit also knows how hard it is for me to know the truth of it all, and still be a witness to what comes from the ignorance of those who will not see.

To put it simply, every day I watch the same people getting stuck in the mud on the same road, in the same places, and then raising hell and whining, and carrying on about their bad luck.

It's this. In a nutshell.

Spirit says:

If your life is in turmoil, and yet you make no changes in that life, then all you can expect is more of the same.

I am often chastised by some for not caring - that because I don't stand in anger and rage, and complain about what they see is wrong, that I'm failing those in need. That I'm some stupid pacifist who's ignoring injustice.

They wave their flags of righteousness in my face.

They are ready for war, and protest, and more violence.

What they don't get is that violence won't change what's wrong, and that stepping onto the path of someone else's tragedy is actual interference. We're not supposed to be owning other people's despair.

I'm not turning a blind eye to the tragedies. I pray for them. But I will not. Do not. Am not, supposed to take on their grief.

Doing that brings other people's turmoil into MY world. Into MY family. And it takes away the peace I work so hard to facilitate within my own world.

Again, I give you a simple analogy.

Taking all of the grief that comes from the great tragedy of others, is like bringing a ticking bomb into your own home. What was peaceful within your world is now fraught with tension, and anger, and fear, because you changed. You changed the dynamic of your personal life by owning someone else's tragedy, and now you are depressed, or consistently angry.

You either take your anger out on the people you love, or you shut down and are no longer available to them. The bomb you brought home WILL go off. When it does you have created your own drama and grief.

And so it is.

Sent with peace.
    Sent with light.
    Sent with love.

Spirit says that man dilutes the words of God to suit himself.

Yes, history may have recorded the edicts of the Great I Am, but often, the defining words that came with them have been changed, or omitted, to suit the purpose of the ruling class of those times.

. . .

Spirit is not happy that man uses God's words as threats.

Or that man has taken it upon himself to 'speak for God."

That man is interpreting God's words to suit his own purposes, and to control the people receiving them.

You don't have to believe in God to know that you are forever in His grace. You don't have to follow a certain path on earth to 'deserve' his love. You have it forever because you are a part of Him.

Spirit says:

God does not show favor to any one belief, because the beliefs, and divisions, and the rules of each sect, have been created by man.

Man has created the divisions.

Man has taken it upon himself to speak for God.

Spirit says:

"Know this. No holy mantle man bestows upon himself or upon another, has any more favor in the eyes of God, than the rags and the lifestyle of the beggar who lives beneath a bridge."

We are all God's children. Pieces of Him. Energy from The Source. From The Universe. No light in heaven shines brighter than another, but for the Light of God. Therefore, no soul who comes here burns brighter than another. It's what you do as human that colors how others see your light.

And so it is.

Sent with peace.
> Sent with light.
> Sent with love.

Options:
  Choices:
  Decisions:
  Spirit says: sometimes your only option is forward, but if you have choices, then only you can make the decision as to which one to make.

  This is life in a nutshell. Often confusing. Constantly evolving.

  And every day you make a choice to participate in one way or another.

This morning, I did not want to participate in anything. I just wanted to stay in bed and sleep. But, I got up anyway, because that's how life works.

  You don't have to 'want' to do something before you begin it.

  You choose to do it.

  You make a decision to do what needs to be done, and that is not an option, that is a responsibility.

  It's called, being an adult.

  It's part of life.

  And today I adulted myself out of bed, and so it goes.

Spirit knows our hearts, and our troubles, and hears our prayers for help.

  And while we're praying to be rescued from our own decisions, what we'll get is the strength to do it ourselves.

  THAT is the true relationship between heaven and earth.

  They never interfere in the free will we came with.

  It's part of the deal.

  They are always the backup. The guidance. They are also the hesitation we feel, asking ourselves is this right? Should we be doing this?

  But the ultimate option, the choice, the decision, is always ours.

. . .

Sent with peace,
   Sent with light.
   Sent with love.

❧

Spirit says:

To find what's missing in your life, first look for what's out of place.

Is your focus on the wrong things?

In this instance, I think a good example of Spirit's point is this:

Do you care more for what others think about you, than how you are perceived by your family?

Are you fun and friendly and outgoing in public, and then turn into a nitpicking, critical human at home?

If this is what's been happening to you, then there is something missing within you, and you've been using the false sense of friendship to fill you up, when it should be the stability, and love of family, that is your life anchor.

If you are someone who has cut all ties with family, and for reasons that are truly healthy FOR YOU, then you have to look elsewhere for what's missing.

Everyone needs an anchor of some kind, even if it's just their own emotional guidance system in good working order, and the easiest way to fill up the well that is YOUR soul, is to do for others, without notice, without fanfare, without telling anyone.

You do it for you, knowing that when your day is over, you have made a difference in another person's life.

Spirit says service to others is vital to humanity.

Find your passion, and you will find your bliss.

And when you do, the change you make in the world around you. Within your workplace. Within your family, will be impossible to miss.

Sent with peace.
   Sent with light.
   Sent with love.

Spirit says:

Feeling all of the emotions of being human is how we work.

Denying how someone or something made you feel, is hurtful to your soul, and to your heart.

If you've been wounded by words, feel the pain, grieve them, and the people who said them, then let them go.

They do not define who YOU are.

They only define the person who spoke them.

Spirit said the people who need this today can gain comfort if they see it, so if it does not apply to you, maybe share it.

Somewhere, there are people right now who have just been hurt deeply by the words of a friend, or a family member, and this is for them - to understand that what was said to them is not THEIR personal truth. Only the perceptions of the people who said them.

Walk away.

Let them be.

They are in their own emotional struggle, and taking it out on you.

Sent with peace.

Sent with light.
Sent with love.

&

I bought a new king-size mattress today. This is my last night to sleep on the old one. They're delivering tomorrow afternoon. I've had this since 2004. That's 15 years, which was before Bobby died.

Right before I had my hip replacement surgery in 2016, I bought one of those ultra- thick mattress pads. It came in a tube shaped thingy from Amazon, and when I started opening it in the living room, it was so compacted in the plastic, that it blew itself out of the packaging, and unfolded to normal size so fast I couldn't get out of the way.

Holy shit, Sherlock!

I kid you not, that was something to experience.

The mattress pad unfolded was really heavy. It wouldn't slide on the laminate flooring because - foam rubber - laminate - non-existent drag effect.

I couldn't walk on it because it was right before my hip replacement, and I hurt too much for all that stumbling and crawling. It was half on the floor and the rest of it splayed out across the end of the dining table and three chairs.

Couldn't even see the freaking floor.

Couldn't get around it.

Couldn't climb over it.

So I went back into the office behind me and called my kids.

Yes, they laughed their asses off at me, but they did get it into my bedroom and onto my old mattress. But putting it on my bed made the mattress so high I couldn't get into bed without steps.

Try bailing out of that kind of bed in a hurry to go pee, and still holding it when you forget the steps, and hit the floor hard and flat-footed. Yeah....that.

So, four years later, the mattress pad, the old mattress, and the bed springs are making an exit tomorrow. And the dudes will set up the new stuff for me, and with box springs that are called low frames, so that my bed's not so high.

I kept calling them low riders, then remembered those are motorcycles, and that was in my youth, and this is a new bed low enough for an old woman to get in and out of without a set of steps.

Tomorrow should be interesting.

And there will be NO need for exploding mattress pads.

※

My mind is in a jumble.

The empath in me has a strong need to withdraw.

This is not a good day for communicating for me.

I have days like this, and my desire to crawl into a hole somewhere, and sleep until the feeling inside me goes away, is strong.

But morning is here. A deadline is near. My head is throbbing from someone else's pain, and I'm tired to the bone of hateful, stupid, people.

There, I said it.

Not sorry.

My truth.

And...Spirit is talking, talking, talking...until I pass on the messages, they won't let me be.

Spirit says:

Look past the obvious.

Stop believing the first thing you read that fits how you think.

Know that your truth and beliefs can be someone else's nightmare.

If you support people who deceive, it is your free will to do so, but remember that also makes you are part of the whole.

Accept that when their lies are revealed, you will be tarnished, too.

My first instinct is to let those people go down with the dark ones, because I reject that kind from my personal space. I want nothing to do with them. I want no conversation to pass between us, because their spirits are like viruses - attacking the weak - ravaging the whole.

But Spirit won't let me go. Spirit won't ignore the hateful and ignorant, even when I want to.

Spirit knows people can change.

Spirit is about saving humanity, while I'm done with most of it.

But my job is my job, and I am a messenger, and so it is.

Being human is different from being in Spirit, and this human life has sucked me dry of patience for people who would be cruel.

You reveal your true selves by what you laugh at, and what you say, and what your write. I see past your physical appearance to the heart beneath. I see you. Every dark thing you advocate is there for me to feel, and my first instinct is to run. That's how strongly hate and racism affect me.

But I stay because Spirit asks.

And I pass Spirit's messages to you because I promised, so I did.

May it fall on the ears of those who need it most.

May it open the eyes of those who refuse to see truth.

May it bring a measure of peace somewhere - anywhere.

Sent with peace.
Sent with light.
Sent with love.

Spirit says:
Shallow people live shallow lives, like gnats skirting across the surface of stagnant water. They are as a nuisance, picking at us, causing just enough trouble so that you know they're there, but disappearing from your lives just in time to save themselves.

Spirit says now is an important time to weed out those who do not serve the purposes you hold true. It's like hanging screens over open windows to keep out the flies.

Now is the time to protect yourself from the liars and the cheats.

Now is the time to look deeper into who you are.

Now is the time to stop laughing at other people's expense.

If you have settled for less, then that will be your life. Less than you were meant to have.

If you have become someone who expects, but does not give in return, then you are less than the person you were meant to be.

If you are someone who spends their last dollar without thinking about tomorrow first, then you are that gnat - skirting the surface of life - hoping for a handout - angry at the world when you don't get it.

Spirit says if this is you, know that you still have within you the power to do better. To be better.

Free will means you've made the choices that got you where you are, and it is free will and new choices that are the means to changing.

It's up to you.

Sent with peace.
    Sent with light.
    Sent with love.

Spirit says:
Choosing to be the best that you can be is hard.
It often means setting aside the sadness, or the difficulties you are facing, and moving through them with a calm you do not feel.
It's life asking you to persevere with grace.
It is possibly the most difficult thing we're ever asked to do.
It is possible.
But it is also free will.
You have to choose to do it.

Sent with peace.
    Sent with light.
    Sent with love.

Spirit says:
When you are born, you are not new. Only the earthly body you have been given in this present lifetime is raw and fresh, waiting to be shaped by the life you will be living.
You are forever.
You are eternal souls who did not originate here, and being afraid of what you don't remember is okay, because your souls know where you belong.
Inanimate things that you own are transient.

They aren't monuments to your lives.

They don't define what you have accomplished or who you are.

In the vernacular of the Universe, you are the present generations, and that is all.

The cycle of life and building, and destruction and birthing, and dying and crying has been happening on this small planet for thousands and thousands of years - farther back than even man now knows.

You are unique to this moment in time, but not to history.

So take what you have and be alive in the moments.

Savor the laughter, and the friendships, the endings and the beginnings, and the constant evolution that is you.

Don't dwell on what was.

It's never coming back.

See what is.

Anticipate what's coming.

Fear nothing.

You are forever.

Sent with peace.
 Sent with light.
 Sent with love.

ॐ

Every dream I have had for weeks is like something is stuck on rewind. No matter what the dream is about, there will be a point where it stops. And then I just go back and begin reliving that same dream, exactly as it was before, even though it won't progress past that last scene. And so it just repeats over and over in my sleep until I wake up.

EVERY. SINGLE. NIGHT.

. . .

Spirit says that's because we're all in a holding pattern. We can't go forward just yet, until the last of the past lets us go. We're not holding onto the past. The past is holding onto us.

It's in our DNA. It's the history of our soul on earth. It's an old way trying to die, and we're all sitting at our own bedsides. watching our pasts letting go.

But it's not death of our physical bodies.

It's the end of a way of life.

Spirit says think of it as the same kind of change as the tiny fertile egg in one woman can turn into a whole other human.

As a caterpillar turns into a butterfly.

What was, becomes something else.

And that's what's happening everywhere.

The old ways no longer serve us. In fact, the old ways rarely served us. We were the servants, doing the bidding and the serving of those who controlled us.

That's part of what's dying.

We may have waited too long to save Earth, but Spirit is saving the human race from extinction.

And as we deny one way, it makes room for new to come in.

Death isn't about ceasing to exist.

It is just existing in a whole other way.

Spirit says you can't stop what's happening now.

To stop fretting about what is not yours to control.

To let go of your fears of the unknown.

At this time on earth, you cannot manifest destiny.

It is in a limbo of its own.

Await what comes with the peace God leaves within us.

Know that you are surrounded with the light of hope for what comes.

Sit witness to the past, but let it go.

Spirit says, it no longer serves you.

Sent with peace.
    Sent with light.
    Sent with love.

       ❧

It's a dreary rainy day here in central Oklahoma, but that's not a complaint. Just an observation. We were in dire need of rain before this rainy spell began last week, and I am grateful for the moisture.

Spirit's message today is about grief, and a reminder that loss is part of living a life.

As humans, letting go is one of the most difficult things we have to experience. We have this innate need to keep - even things that do not serve us. We accumulate. We hoard.

And that includes letting go of people.

Some come into our lives but for a short while.

They were here for a reason, but were never meant to stay.

And some are here for the long haul.

But the time will inevitably come when we have to accept that their journey here is ending, and that their paths and ours are now going in different directions.

And this is when it's time to let go.

Spirit says, do not claim their passing as the face you must wear for the rest of your life.

It is not your duty to be the grief-holder for the rest of YOUR life.

When we lose an elderly loved one, we're thinking only of our loss. It never occurs to us to acknowledge that, once upon a time when they were young, they lost loved ones, too. That they buried their parents and siblings and friends, and they grieved. And then they went on to live the lives into which you were born. You only knew them from your perspective. You never think that they might be looking forward to rejoining their loved ones in spirit. You don't think of them as getting to go home. You think of them as having disappeared, because you can no longer see or hear them.

Spirit says:

Take heart. They haven't gone far. They are always within the sound of your voice. When you speak their names they smile. When you laugh from the memories of times you spent together, they are laughing with you.

They will be with you always, and waiting to hold your hand when it is time to come home.

Sent with peace.
    Sent with light.
    Sent with love.

Spirit sends this message.
    You are addicted to technology.
    It is your drug.
    It must be in your hands, or plugged into your ears.
    You are not looking up. You are not paying attention.
    You do not see each other anymore.
    You are losing your ability to verbally communicate.

There is an entire generation of people who already cannot spell, or do math without technology.

You think you are so new, and so current.

You think your ability to use technology, and your ability to program it makes you special.

You have no idea that by giving up your sovereignty to the world wide web, that you also gave up your privacy, and your lives.

You bought into the idea of better being easier.

You took the shortcuts to success.

And now every piece of you is in someone else's hands.

They track you. Every day. Everywhere.

Spirit says because you have chosen this way, that it will be on you to accept the consequences when it all fails.

Being angry won't change it.

Then you will look up.

But you won't know the faces of the people before you.

And you will be in a land of strangers just like you.

It will be because you chose this.

And so it is.

Sent with peace.
> Sent with light.
> Sent with love.

&

Spirit says:

A lie, is a lie, is a lie.

Spreading misinformation is as damaging to society, as a chemical spill in water is to the life within it.

It's all poison. It was all caused by humans. And you have only yourselves to blame for the discord.

Spirit says: Discord has become the norm when there is murder all around us, and people argue over the type of weapons used to cause it...and feel no empathy for the lives that were lost.

When this happens, you have lost your humanity.

When you lose the concept of humanity, then it is doomed to fail.

Once, it was dangerous to live alone, or in small families on this vast continent, and so people began congregating into larger, and larger, communities until they became cities. And they let themselves become submissive to a ruler. And then they lost their sovereignty, and became slaves ,and chattel, to their Kings and Warlords.

And now it is more dangerous to live together in large cities than it is to live alone, or in small families back out on the land. Even enduring personal hardships is more enticing to some, than to be afraid of the person passing you on the street.

Spirit says what was, is returning to what will be, because of the free will of humanity.

You destroyed yourselves.

And now this destruction is part of the rebuilding - rebirthing, and you will wake up, and you will have a choice to make.

You will either choose a new way on earth, or choose to stay behind with what you broke, and what you killed, and all of what you've wrought.

And so it is.

Sent with peace.
    Sent with light.
    Sent with love.

Spirit says:

Walk in truth.

There is no need to hide a sadness, or an anger. Live it. Feel it. Then find a way to let it go.

In life, pretending to be one way, and living another, is living a lie.

Lies are wounds.

They can scab over...and you can almost forget you told it, until someone uses your lie as a fact. As a truth. And passes it on.

At that point, the scab comes off, and you remember.

That's when true guilt sets in. Then you regret ever saying it, but you let it live, because it's easier than admitting your mistake.

Imagine living an entire lifetime wearing a mask.

Never revealing how you really look. How you feel. How you think.

Always going along with the herd because you're afraid to be different. Afraid of your own sovereignty. Afraid. Afraid. Afraid. But of what? Of your own truth?

Spirit says:

Humanity depends upon the truth seekers. The truth speakers. And living any other way but in your own truth brings you down into darkness.

Spirit says standing in truth is standing in light.

And standing in God-light is the safest, truest place on earth you can be.

Sent with peace.

Sent with light.

Sent with love.

Spirit says:

Even in the darkest of times, YOUR light never goes out.
It's what some people call strength.
What others call faith.
But it doesn't need to be identified to use it.
Spirit reminds you:

Soul light is God-light. God is within you always. Even when you are wrong. Even when you have committed great sins. Even then, you are still one of HIS.

We have laws to follow, and if we break them, then punishment is due.

It is our way.

But if the only complaint you feel toward another is based on a personal opinion, then you have stepped into a place in which you are not supposed to be.

If someone displeases you, then that is your burden to deal with.

They are not here to make your life pleasant and perfect.

They are on a mission of their own, of which you know nothing about.

Judging others is not for us.

Judgment is left up to God.

Spirit empathizes with our fears. They are understood, but at the same time, all that is happening here that we are caught up in, is happening because of personal choices others made - and we have become caught up in the storm front of the chaos they have created.

None of this is God's doing. God isn't destroying us, or Mother Earth.

We did it to ourselves.

And neither God, nor his angels, will interfere with the free will of man.

It is part of the deal we made when we came here. And the sooner you understand that praying to be rescued from your own mistakes isn't going to happen, the sooner you will figure out how to fix what you broke, and save yourself.

. . .

Our lives were mapped out before we came.

I don't know why I thought it would be a good idea to endure all that I have gone through in my life, but I accept the truth that I did agree. And I know when I do go home, that all will be revealed to me.

What I don't want, is to go back having failed in the promises I made, and the duties I did not fulfill.

So when times get hard, and sad, and life bitch-slaps me enough to make me mad. I still don't quit on God, because He'll never quit on me.

Sent with peace.
    Sent with light.
    Sent with love.

As an empath, my heart hurts daily for those who are suffering.

And because of all the little pitfalls and turmoil happening in my own personal space, I missed the real reason for my deepest despair.

Never in my lifetime have I witnessed such blatant disregard for law, for human suffering, for giving up our sovereignty to a despot, and his pack.

I am not apolitical....I am not a believer of sects, or of the separation of people because of religions, or ethnicity, although that's what we have become.

But I am a person who believes in a humanitarian way of life.

Everybody eats. Everybody has care and medical treatments. Everybody has shelter and a measure of safety.

This is how I believe the world should be...and we should not have to die to attain this level of love for one another.

Normally, I try to protect myself from whatever is happening, that is not mine to suffer.

But my own personal turmoil distracted me enough that I realized last night I was letting myself be pulled into the physical energy of a worldwide grief.

It is the suffering that I feel.

The children ripped away from their parents.

The people of Puerto Rico who were abandoned.

The Bahamian people who have been abandoned.

The children who disappear into the world of human trafficking.

The evil we do to each other.

The blind eye we turn to lies.

Our refusal to see or hear a truth.

The mass murders that have become our norm.

The children who are now afraid to go to school.

And on...and on...and on...into the evil being done in the name of power and greed.

Spirit says the truth of those in power is measured by their obvious inhumanity to those in need.

Spirit says: They are the antithesis of the only thing that was asked of us in heaven before we incarnated here as human.

"To love one another as I have loved you. To do unto others, as you would have them do unto you."

Spirit says: Those who accept their evil as righteous, fall short in the eyes of God. That you are setting the course for your own spiritual downfall. That you will not attain or complete in this lifetime, the lessons you came to learn, or the purposes for which you were meant to achieve. That you have stepped off the path of God into the world of darkness.

Spirit says. And so it is. And so it will be.

. . .

Sent with peace.
   Sent with light.
   Sent with love.

༄

Spirit says the phrase, All is lost, is being misinterpreted.

ALL is NEVER lost, because life never ends. It only shifts into another dimension.

Spirit also says that humanity cares more for the loss of structures, and lifestyles, and belongings, than they do the lives of people they do not know.

We are so overwhelmed by the daily travesty and tragedies befalling us now, that we are becoming immune to the shock of it.

Oh, another hurricane. Oh, another earthquake - just look at the destruction. Oh, another mass shooting incident. Let's fight over guns, and ignore the people who died, and the families in grief. Let's argue about the size of the gun, instead of the baby someone now has to bury, because it's easier to fight than it is to face the inhumanity of man.

Let's all cry out in unison: "Someone needs to do something. I know. I'll say prayers." And then let's all look away and let it be.

Until it happens to you. Until you are the one who's child went missing. Who's daughter disappeared. Who's son went down with a ship. Who's grandparents were swept off an island, and out into the sea. Until it's personal.

Then you want justice for their murders, or you want them to be saved, and to be found. Then the someone who needs to do something is you, and you want everyone to care, but they're not in your personal space. They're out there where you were, before you became the victim.

Spirit says: Everyone matters equally. And care for all should come as a matter of course, not on a pick and choose basis.

Spirit says...until you put all life on the same plane of importance, you are not living at an ascending level of light and energy, and in the days to come, that is going to matter.

Sent with peace.
    Sent with light.
    Sent with love.

⁂

Most times, honesty makes people uncomfortable.
    So we keep our truth to ourselves.
    When the only person who can hear what you're thinking is God, at least you know your truth will not show up on Social Media.

The irony of their discomfort is that they continue telling their troubles to the world, but in their minds, that's different.
    In their need to be heard, they spread their truth near and far, then wait for responses that back them up, and fight with people who disagree.
    They want to be heard, but they don't want to listen to anyone else.

Because we are human, we hurt.
    When we need help, we reach out.
    And when help doesn't come, we feel rejected and angry, and we hurt even more.

And so the cycle continues and grows with no resolution, and causes anger and despair.

And if nothing changes, then you have to be the one to change it.

Spirit says:

The greatest failing of being human is lack of compassion for others.

But there again, compassion alone solves nothing.

It is only an emotion. And people who are sad, are already full of their own emotions, so they don't need or want that pat on the head, or that empty hug - and the empty byword so popular now - I'll pray for you.

People who are sad need what made them sad to be resolved.

That's what they want. That's all they need. Even when they're not going to get it. And so they grieve for what was.

Spirit says:

The actual act of prayer has become contaminated by the pseudo-use of placating.

You say you'll do it - so in your mind you've already done it just by saying - you're in my prayers.

BUT - Are you down on your knees saying those people's names aloud, beseeching the Great I Am for intercession on their behalf - or do you consider it already done?

Spirit says:

Therein lies the deterioration of the meaning.

Yes, sometimes truth hurts. And sometimes life hurts us.

And we are allowed to be sad any way we feel the need to express it. It is no one else's business. If they don't like it, they are free to move along.

. . .

Spirit says:

It is your human right to feel your own grief in the way it best serves you, because you cannot move through grief, until you have acknowledged it is there.

Sent with peace.
Sent with light.
Sent with love.

❦

You don't have to be Native American to receive their wisdom.
They are Keepers of The Earth. The Sky. The Wind. The Water.
Their wisdom is meant for us all.
You don't have to be African to receive the wisdom of their culture.
You don't have to be Jewish to receive the wisdom of their culture.
You don't have to be Asian to receive the wisdom of their culture.
And so it goes. For every culture. For as long as time, it's the wisdom of the ages that rings true for all of us.
And when you belittle and besmirch another race through prejudice, and color all of them because of the sins of the few, that fault lies with you, not them.
Spirit says:
Our souls are all God-light. In the eyes of the great I AM, we are all alike because we all come from Source.
There is no distinction of color, appearance, sex, or status...only the light within us.
If you covered your light in this lifetime to chase that which did not serve your purpose, then it is your light that will reveal your truth. Either it grew brighter, stronger, and absorbed all that it was meant to see and need. Or, you let it grow dim.

You cannot lie to Source. You cannot spin your tale of who's fault - or not my fault. All will be revealed, and you will either ascend in grace, or you will return to make right the things you did wrong.

Atoning is a long and emotional journey.

The consequences of the blind eye you turned here will be revealed to you, and the shame you feel will be real.

Spirit says: And so it is.

Sent with peace.

Sent with light.

Sent with love.

I dreamed all night...hopping from one thing to another.

That's how dreams are.

Sometimes they are triggered by people or events happening to you.

Sometimes they are old memories, and sometimes fear of the unknown of what's coming.

They are your subconscious self, and they are soul memories.

And for some of us, messages.

Mine was a message.

When trust is gone, awareness rises.

Spirit says:

The biggest deceptions you will ever experience are when you deceive yourself.

It's when you want something bad enough to ignore all of the signs, and all of your inner warning signals, and let it happen.

At that point, you own what comes.

You bought it - you sold your honor - your dignity - and sometimes your own people for selfish reasons.

Sent with peace.

Sent with light.
Sent with love.

⁂

Spirit says:
Everything changes. Without change there can be no growth.

As a farmer's child, and then a farmer's wife, my life - my world - was timed by seasons. Spring planting, summer crops and canning, fall harvest getting in the last crops. Then winter. The time for earth to rest while man still toils. Responsibilities continue regardless of life and weather.

Now my life has nothing to do with seasons, just deadlines. From one book to another. Day in and day out. Still working with my hands. Still growing from my imagination and dreams. Still harvesting every time a book is released for sale.

And such is life.

Spirit says:
A shallow life is but a half-life. Without experiencing the depths of emotions. The highs and the lows. Appreciation for the good times is taken for granted.

Sent with peace.
Sent with light.
Sent with love.

⁂

Spirit says:
Your first thought should be a positive one.
Your last thought should be accepting what is.
After that, it is possible to move forward.

We all do what we feel is right to serve our purpose.

It's when we do something harmful to others, in the process to gain what we want, that changes us - changes who we were meant to be, and what we came here to do.

The world is full of people wanting the same things you want, and having their own right to seek them.

It's NEVER just about you.

Yes, chase your dreams.

But first - do no harm.

Sent with peace.
   Sent with light.
   Sent with love.

Spirit says:
Be kind to the child in you.
Remind him/her they are loved.
Do one thing per day that is for you alone.
It is not selfish to think of yourself.
You can't share love, until you have it to give.

Sent with peace.
   Sent with light.
   Sent with love.

Spirit says:
Every morning there is a light in the sky that takes us through

our day.

Even when it's hidden behind storm clouds, or an overcast sky, it's still there.

That's how God is.

Even when we won't acknowledge Him - He's still there loving us.

Shine your light.

Be the light for someone else who's having a gray day.

There are shadows in everyone's life from time to time.

Some are darker. Some linger longer. But they always pass.

Just keep moving forward.

Sent with peace.
Sent with light.
Sent with love.

Spirit says:
Patience is required today.

Be at peace with what is, or set right that which does not please you in a calm, but righteous, manner. Anger is not necessary when you state your choice, and walk away from discord.

I thought of making taffy with my Grand the other day. She used to make it a lot when we were little. It's quite a process, but the end result was such a treat.

I think we liked the candy most because of the delight we got in getting to help pull it when it was ready.

It couldn't be too hot to handle, but you had to do it while it was still warm, or it would get too hard to pull - and pulling was what turned it from a clear thick liquid, to a near-white, sticky, chewy, creamy bite.

Grand would dump the warm taffy candy out onto large platter. We had to butter our hands before we started, and then she picked it up in one lump and give it a pull.

She'd hand one end of the long loop to me, or to my Grampy, and then we'd pull away from her, but not enough to make it pull apart. Then we'd quickly put the two ends together again, make a new loop and pull, working it this way over and over and over, until the taffy was twice the size from when we'd started, and it had lost it's clear shiny luster, from the air we'd worked into it.

About every five or ten pulls, Grand would also give it a twist it in mid-air, like she was braiding it, then keep pulling.

After a while, the candy was no longer clear, and was turning a thick, creamy white. If Grand had put a drop or two of peppermint oil into it as it was cooling, then she usually put a drop of red food coloring, too. So we always knew the pink taffy was peppermint. The white taffy was vanilla.

The fun part was when it finally got to the right stage for cutting.

I never could tell, but Grand knew by the feel of the taffy.

At that point, Grampy would get the big kitchen shears, and we'd pull a strand longer and slimmer, and he'd snip it off in small pieces onto wax paper.

Grand was all business.

Grampy was all about the tasting.

After it was all cut, we'd wrap each piece in a little twist of waxed paper, and put it in her crystal candy dish with the domed lid. She would set it on the end of the kitchen counter where it was within grandkid reach, and handy for Grampy to take a piece with him on the way out the door.

This was such a simple pleasure, and something that has become a lost art. But that also describes the things I value most - the simple things - the memories - and all that love and laughter.

Sticky candy. Sticky fingers. Sticky kisses. Lots of love.

Be grateful for each day.

Life does not come with promises.

. . .

Sent with peace.
    Sent with light.
    Sent with love.

Spirit says:

Give with the expectation of never getting it back, or never give at all.

If you give and expect return, then you spend your life begrudging your generosity.

You hold hard feelings for the ones who never pay it back.

Seek your friends among the ones who know how to share their joy without grudging you a smile.

The ones who delight in your laughter.

The ones who care about you, too, and not just themselves.

The ones who demand nothing of you.

The ones who allow you the freedom of giving of yourself.

And so it is.

On another note:

My daughter's little King Charles Spaniel, Winston Miller, doesn't just bark. He also chirps. Highest pitched yips ever. Winston is chirping now because his Mama (my daughter) and his boy (my grandson, Scout) are in the garage, and he is not.

And he is NOT with them because the other day he pranced himself out and across the street before his Mama could catch him, and he found himself face to face with a towering, black German Shepherd.

His Mama said he went head down. Belly flat, tail tucked between his legs as the monster sniffed him. He was not harmed in any way, but it scared the bejesus out of him. He ran back so fast that, by the time his Mama caught him, he dropped flat on the concrete, and couldn't bring himself to walk.

He'd scared himself so bad that, despite her bad back, she had to pick him up and carry him back into the house.

So now he comes into my office, and sits behind my chair when I'm working. The windows are almost floor to ceiling, so he looks out across the street at where the giant lives - and growls.

Sometimes, the monsters in your mind aren't really monsters at all, but the manifestations of your own fears.

That's when you are called upon to go to battle for yourself.

Face what you fear most and find a way to conquer it.

That's a part of life.

Correcting mistakes.

Figuring it out.

Sent with peace.
Sent with light.
Sent with love.

ૈ

Spirits says:

That which you think about, talk about, focus on, is what you draw to you.

If you aren't careful, you can become a perpetual victim.

You begin to identify as 'that person'. The one who- Or the person who was- Or the person who's family did- Or the child of- The wife of-

You take on the guilt of someone else by association, and that is not your burden to bear or share.

. . .

It can also happen when you can't let go of a disagreement you had with someone, then the energy of that anger stays with you, and spreads to others as you move through a day.

And by the same token, being around someone else who is angry or disgruntled will affect you, in the same way you might have affected others.

Think of yourself as the light you are.

Now think of how hard it would be to keep that light lit while standing in a storm.

Negative people create their own storms.

It is on you to find a way out and free yourself.

When you surround yourself with good people who mean you no harm, their energy feeds the energy you use to keep your light from going dim.

Think of them as the globe around your light, helping you keep it lit.

Think of joy - even if you can't feel it.

Think of peace - even when you're still seeking it.

Think of light - even if yours seems dim.

Think of love - even if it eludes you.

Because Spirit says:

That which you think about, you draw to you.

Spirit says:

There is always an answer.

It may not be the one you asked for, but it is the answer.

Proceed as you will.

I don't dwell on the days of my loved ones' passing. But they are always in my heart - some days stronger than others, and that's okay, but it doesn't mean it's time to retrieve old grief.

It's just a nudge from Spirit to rejoice that they were here.

. . .

If you have grown into the adult your parents wanted you to be, then you do not need their physical presence to live out the rest of your life.

I tell my children this all the time. I want them to remember their own power. I want them to be happy in their own lives, just as my parents learned how to be after their parents were gone, and so it goes.

From as far back in time as there has been life, there has also been loss.

Our grief is not new. Yes, it is our grief, and we're allowed to feel it, but there comes a time when you will also release it.

Grief is not meant to stay with us.

It is transient.

Memories are ours forever.

Hold them close, and when the need arises, take them out and laugh again. Cry again. And release again.

Because in life, everything always comes full circle.

Sent with peace.
    Sent with light.
    Sent with love.

Spirit says:
    You are a sovereign soul.
    Your power is eternal.
    It does not change from lifetime to lifetime.
    You are always - in every incarnation - the same soul forever.
    Remember that.

. . .

Remember that you have succeeded and failed, and loved and lost in many other lifetimes, and nothing that's happening to you now is new.

Maybe this life you're living now is just something that you are still learning how to navigate.

Or you have come here as a teacher, and have willingly chosen to experience this life in whatever forms it takes, to stand as an example of how to navigate trouble - how to survive hard times.

Some of us learn by doing.
    Others learn by watching someone else demonstrate the process.
    And so it is with each life we live.
    Sometimes we are learning.
    Sometimes we are teaching.
    But we are always growing. It is the way of the soul - to cycle from one life to another until it has grown in such light and grace and majesty that it has ascended and transcended into a dimension beyond human understanding.

Sent with peace.
    Sent with light.
    Sent with love.

༄

I Am In Transition:
After the fourteen years of caring for my mother, who suffered from dementia - after the ten years I kept her with me in my home - after the four years she was in memory care before she passed in November 2018 because I could no longer keep her safe - I am basically bankrupt and losing my home. I mortgaged my car to

pay for her last month of care before she died, and have been living on credit cards for her care, and juggling payments for her and my life, the last two years. Until I dropped all of the balls at once, and so it is.

Health care in America is appalling. For the elderly, it is a joke, and families pay, and families lose.

I tell you this, so that you can better understand the tone of the posts that follow this.

This isn't fishing for pity.

This isn't an excuse for anything.

I did what I did for her out of love, because she would have done it for me.

But I am struggling with Spirit and staying upbeat.

I feel abandoned.

And there are days I feel betrayed by a host of people I thought I could count on.

But life is about teaching moments, and these past months have taught me plenty.

I have a son, a daughter, and four grandchildren who love me, and that sustains me.

And so it is.

❦

This morning, Spirit showed me a vision.
I knew what it was.
The Cherokee walking the Trail of Tears.

A reminder that people - my ancestors - were once uprooted from their lives, and everything they had was taken away from them.

They had no shelter.

They had few horses.

They were driven away from their lands, and their homes, and their crops, and their livestock.

Taking only what they could carry, they were marched away

from their homes by force, driven out by soldiers, because the government wanted their land, and took it.

Old and young, weak and strong, sick and the dying...it didn't matter.

Their journey was hard - and it was long.

Many died, and some survived.

I am here because a woman on that walk did not quit.

I am here because a man who's blood I share, kept putting one foot in front of the other.

I am here because some died for me.

I am here.

I am many things. But I carry the blood and the DNA of the Cherokee, and the Old Ones are with me. I carry the blood if the Cree, and I will not fail.

The Guardians surround me when I am in need of strength.

I am sad, but I do not walk their Trail of Tears.

My ancestors already walked it for me.

So this is what I saw. This is what I know.

Every day we have the option to keep putting one foot in front of the other.

Or quit.

I never quit.

And Spirit just reminded me why this trait is within me.

I have often been forced to readjust.

During the hardships of this past years, I have lost my sense of safety.

Nothing is certain anymore.

But I am still here.

And that's all I have to know.

Sent with peace.
Sent with light.
Sent with love.

It rained most of the night and into the morning. Still misting. Very cold and windy.

I ran errands this morning and am in the house, beyond grateful for shelter.

I dreamed all night of people who didn't keep their word, and people who went off and left me.

Just a side-effect of all that has happened.

This too shall pass.

I have no control over other people's words and actions.

Only the manner in which I choose to receive it.

Spirit says:

Choice is part of your free will. You are never forced. You may give into pressure. You may let someone else speak for you. You may even choose to follow the crowd. But in any case, making no choice IS a choice to allow the status quo to continue.

When my children were little, we always made caramel apples. It was a thing that started with my mother. It was such a treat to have them, and fun to make them, too.

Mother would buy four big beautiful apples, a little package of Popsicle sticks, and a big bag of Kraft caramels.

My sister, Diane, and I got the job of unwrapping the caramels, and promising not to eat more than a couple apiece, so we'd have enough to melt and dip the apples.

The smell of warm caramel, the crisp apples freshly washed and waiting to be dipped, and the cozy little kitchen in the house where I grew up was such a sweet memory, that I carried it over into my house when I became a mother.

My children became the official peelers of caramels. I poked

Popsicle sticks in the apples, and we dipped them in the warm, melted caramel, then set them aside to cool.

But just like when Diane and I were little, the apples never lasted long. There were never leftovers. We ate them down to the core, still licking at the Popsicle sticks for the lingering flavor of that thick, sweet caramel.

Memories are God-winks. Bits of what a soul deems worth keeping.

But it is up to you as to how you receive them.

Either with regret that time is over - or with gratitude that it ever happened.

Sent with peace.
    Sent with light.
    Sent with love.

Still cold. Still raining.

I'll be writing by the fireplace today.

Tomorrow is the yard sale at my daughter's house.

She is getting rid of what she can't take with her when she and my grandson move in with me. Her life is in transition, too.

She's been selling things along for a couple of weeks now, but tomorrow is the day for selling all of what's left, and hauling the rest away.

Everything there from T-posts, and lumber, and tools, to her kitchen stove, furniture, a window air conditioner, to garden seeds. Anything you can imagine an urban gardener would have been using. As she says.. "Make me an offer."

She will be listing the house for sale soon afterward.

I'm going to be there with her for company and moral support. It's hard to have a sale of that size on your own.

Spirit says:

Sadness and hardship comes to all of us at one time or another, and none of it is generated by God as lesson or punishment. They are things you chose to learn before you came.

The unfortunate part of that message is that we are not allowed to remember our soul lives while we are here. A few do, but it's rare, and there are reasons for that, as well.

And not remembering our choices, makes what's happening to us harder to bear. Sometimes the illnesses and troubles are overwhelming. Some of us break. And some of us don't.

But breaking doesn't mean failure.

Maybe the breaking point WAS the thing you came to learn.

There is always a second way to look at life.

From your perspective, and from the perspective of someone else.

Neither one is wrong, but only one will be right for you.

Spirit says: Judgment is God's right, not yours.

Spirit says: Love each other as the humans you all are.

And so it is.

Sent with peace.
    Sent with light.
    Sent with love.

My ex-husband - my children's father - was killed in a car wreck this afternoon. I am so sad for his wife JoAnn, and for our children and grandchildren. Keep them all in your prayers.

. . .

Spirit says:
>Remember Ecclesiastes 3:
>"There is a time for everything and a season for every activity under the heavens:
>A time to be born and a time to die.
>And so this is brought home to many every day, just as it has been to my family.
>Waste not the chance to make peace.
>Don't leave an apology undone.
>Take time to say I love you.
>That 'time' can be taken away from you in the blink of an eye.
>This has been a hard year, and it just got worse.

Sent with peace.
>Sent with light.
>Sent with love.

Spirit says:

Understanding and kindness are traits that are part of your soul.

We all know people who make you feel welcome.
>Who stand as witness to your troubles without judging...even when they disagree wholeheartedly with your choices.
>The ones who allow everyone the space to tell their story.
>Their instinct is led by the innate sense that comes with soul.
>They don't put labels on people.
>They have learned not to label themselves.
>Often, they are introverts, unwilling to put themselves into the spotlight.
>They are more comfortable with just being -

Than being SEEN, or being KNOWN.

Spirit says:
>Honor the quiet ones.
>Education and knowledge are taught
>Wisdom comes from living life...not from reading books.
>Outrage in its place is understood.
>But you can lose yourself fighting someone else's war.
>Psalm 46:10
>Be still, and know that I am God.

Sent with peace.
>Sent with light.
>Sent with love.

❦

Spirit says:
>**Understanding is not always given.**
>**In those times, you hold onto faith.**

Scout took his Mama to help her step-mother make funeral arrangements for her daddy.
>Her step-mother is exhausted. My daughter is exhausted. She was already so tired from moving, and at this point is in motion from determination alone.
>My son is shattered, too, but a quiet one - like me.
>There to help, but keeping everything inside.
>They're all suffering from the shock and the sadness.
>The tired will go away.
>The sadness eventually changes to something more manageable.
>And life will go on, with one more sweet soul to miss.

. . .

It's very cold and windy here today. I think it's in the 40s, but they said something about a wind chill of 30 degrees.
   Oklahoma and her wind.
   It will cut you like a knife.

Staying in toxic relationships - both with friends, spouses, or life partners - is slow poison.
   When they reveal themselves to you, believe them.
   It is always your choice to keep them within the circle of your life, or not.
   But your life does not revolve around someone else's presence or opinions before it matters...and no one but you can make it work.

I've had plenty of people disapprove of me in my lifetime.
   I've had people trying to tell me what I should do.
   But they haven't lived my life.
   They don't know my story.
   They don't get to be in charge of me.
   Remember your sovereignty.
   Own your autonomy.
   You have the power within you to survive whatever comes, even though there's no way to know an outcome.
   A true warrior faces life.
   Stand up.
   You are ready.

Sent with peace.
   Sent with light.
   Sent with love.

Spirit says:
Love is eternal in spirit.
There are no human traits left in us by the time we are home.
Even though it is difficult to achieve, aspiring to that perfection is part of our human experience.
We came here to learn how to love more. Love harder. Love inclusively.
Whatever we do, or do not, achieve in this lifetime is not success or failure.
It is simply more of the same. Learning the lesson of love.

Sent with peace.
    Sent with light.
    Sent with love.

Spirit says:
Thoughts are your own until you utter them aloud.
Speaking words gives them life.
Once voiced, they can never be unheard.
Whatever was said has been received.
Whether it was helpful, or hurtful, is all on you.

We had a large number of trick-or-treaters last night.
My daughter sat out on the front porch in the cold, with a bowl of candy in her lap to hand out because:
    A. Dogs in the house.
    B. No storm door between people and dogs when the door is open.
    C. Large amounts of barking.

D. Dogs in the house.

We were seriously impressed by the organization of the parents who accompanied these children.
One car driving into the neighborhood ahead of those walking.
Parents walking in front of the kids. With the kids. Behind the kids. And one to two cars driving a distance behind them. They counted heads constantly. And the darker it got, the more concentrated they all became.
And why?
Because of child trafficking.
Because evil lives and walks among us.

Today is a day for finishing up things yet undone.
Scout is home with me. His last day off after the death of his grandfather.
My daughter is on the go because, in death many things are left undone, too, and finishing them up is now her task.

Sent with peace.
Sent with light.
Sent with love.

◆

Spirit says:
In all things, God is uppermost.
It was a really simple statement to get from Spirit this morning, but I never question it. I just post it as I am told.

. . .

In my head...I am thinking to myself...this is just a reminder to keep myself in a place of acceptance for what is.

To remind myself that this life is not about being perfect.

It is about understanding the imperfections.

To remind myself that I have been this way before. In other lives. In other times.

And whatever my fate was then has simply moved me on into this life.

To remind myself that I am not the only one in distress.

To remember that we are all a part of God, and that I choose to follow His commandment

LOVE ONE ANOTHER AS I HAVE LOVED YOU.

Once you lose God in your life, you lose your way.

That doesn't mean He's lost you.

It just means you let go of your strongest anchor.

You are adrift within the chaos of being human.

Be at peace within yourself.

Don't blame.

Don't rage.

Understand that you are not the only one in crisis.

And unless you are asked to help, your opinions are not required.

Sent with peace.
    Sent with light.
    Sent with love.

❧

The lady who helps me clean house is running the vacuum.

Winston Miller, my daughter's little King Charles Spaniel, is hiding behind my office chair.

I smell Winston, and Pet Fresh, all at the same time.

It is an interesting combination.

. . .

We are all in different cycles of good and bad.

We are energetically impacted by the positive, and the negative, around us.

It is up to us to find our place of peace.

Feeling sorry for yourself is human nature.

We all do it.

But wallowing in it gets us nowhere.

Wearing your 'bad luck' badge is not a badge of honor.

It is a sign that you've chosen to blame everyone else for what's happening to you.

It will not be your shining moment.

Free will gives us choices.

If you choose to live life as a victim, then that is certainly your choice, and your right. But expecting others to live that with you isn't fair.

They have their own free will, and choices, and they do not have to coincide with yours, nor is it fair to blame them for rejecting yours.

What you have yet to understand is that YOU weren't rejected. It was the choices you made, and the people and places you chose to inhabit, that put you where you are, and prompted their decisions.

I am an empath.

I feel things from people, even though they are unaware of it.

I know when I'm being used.

I see past your facade to the truth beneath.

You can't fool me with words and smiles.

That I choose to tolerate it is on me. Until I've had enough.

And then I walk away from what offends me.

I walk away from that which threatens me.

I walk away from other people's anger.

I walk away from other peoples lies.

Because this is my life, and my choices, and my free will.

And so it is for you.

Your life.
Your free will.
Your choices.
And your consequences.
Sent with peace.
Sent with light.
Sent with love.

I was running errands this morning when a panhandler in Ace Hardware hit me up for money.

"I've been on the streets for a while now," he said, and I looked into his eyes and saw much suffering. Whatever has happened. Even if he caused it. He was in terrible distress. That's my biggest fear - to wind up homeless. And so

I stood there a few seconds, remembering something my Bobby always said about giving from his heart because he wanted to, without judging what someone else MIGHT do with it - and pulled out money I didn't have to spare, and gave him some anyway.

They ran him out of the store soon afterward, but he went out the door better off than when he came in, and that's all that mattered to me.

If only we all could go through each day knowing we'd end up a little better off than when it began, it would make the hard parts of life easier to bear.

I never thought I'd live to see a time when the average person's attention span was the length of Tweet or a Meme.

I actually saw someone post a question to a friend..."Will it be too long for me to want to read?"

What the actual hell ya'll?

How truly ignorant of the world do you want to be?

. . .

My job as a writer is swiftly falling out of favor.

I hope I'm long dead before people quit reading for pleasure.

I don't think I'd enjoy a society that has lost the joy of imagination, and the ability to get lost in a story.

After all that's happened, I've been disenchanted with life and people in general for quite awhile now. That happens when the world you knew implodes, sinking you with it.

So I'm watching nothing but Food Network, and the Hallmark Channels. If you get enough sweet stuff, and happy ever-afters in your day, it keeps hope afloat.

Spirit says:

Time is eternal, but we are not.

Don't waste what you've been given by wishing for what you don't have.

Sent with peace.
Sent with light.
Sent with love.

It's cold and raining again.
It began yesterday close to sundown.
I was out with some last minute mail for the post office, and saw a homeless woman standing beneath a small gazebo near an old library, taking shelter where she found it. I said a prayer for her and kept driving, because I couldn't take that grief home with me.

When I was a little girl, I loved the rain. It was a day to spend curled up with a book, lost in the story, and living within the pages of the characters' lives.

Books were magic to me then.
I didn't know that I'd been given the magic to make them.

We are all born with gifts. That one was mine.
Some people have been given the gift of teaching.
Some people become healers.
Some people have the gift of being able to take things apart, and put them back together again in working condition.
Some people are naturals at all manner of cooking.
Some people have been given the gift of service to others, which encompasses many occupations, like law enforcement and military, cab drivers, clerks in stores, people who care enough to help in any capacity.
Some people ignore their gifts, and wander aimlessly through life in constant dissatisfaction, and don't know why that aren't happy.
And some souls purposefully choose to live those kinds of lives before they came here. To experience these very things for a greater understanding of the humans who lose their way, and make the terrible choices that set them on paths to destruction.
Living is about learning.
I am grateful for the roof over my head and the warm bed I slept in last night. I am still in search of solace and safety, but today, this is enough.

Sent with peace.
   Sent with light.
   Sent with love.

Spirit says
Do not begin today with yesterday.

It is over.

Don't talk about what was.

Think about what could be.

Just because you are highly educated means you have knowledge, but it does not mean you have wisdom.

Just because you're old, doesn't necessarily mean you are wise.

It takes life, and time, and knowledge, then applying it, to achieve wisdom.

When I was a little girl, my daddy always had a funny joke to tell. Friends and family gathered around him at family events, waiting for Doc, (it was my daddy's nickname) to get wound up, because when he did, laughter flowed.

When my uncles would all started howling and slapping their legs from laughing so hard, invariably one of my aunties would frown and mutter..."That man. Likely, he's telling one of his dirty jokes, again."

Mother would just roll her eyes. There is no conjecture, when a truth is a truth.

But jokes aren't a thing anymore. There are Memes and snark being shared on people's phones, but when they laugh, they laugh alone, because they're the only one seeing it. In one more generation, people will have quit looking at each other when they speak.

Winston Miller is sleeping behind my chair. He likes to curl up beneath the window in my office as I type.

He snores.

But I am safe. So safe. Because Winston Miller's got my back, and Geenie Dog, who belongs to my grandson, Scout, is guarding the front door.

God help me if I need to hurry and go pee, because I'll stumble over dogs to do it, but in the meantime, I am behind great walls of fur and teeth, and when the need arises, also barking. Much barking.

I'm going to work now.

Smashed finger isn't as sore as it was yesterday.

Off to make my own brand of magic.

Telling stories like my Daddy, but without the dirty jokes. Just a curse word or two from a bad guy now and then. Because I am my father's daughter, and that's how I roll.

Sent with peace.
    Sent with light.
    Sent with love.

Spirit says:
    Walk in peace today.
    It matters.

I don't know what this means, but I'm delivering the message. Maybe the choice you make not to argue with someone will be a turning point in your life.

Maybe you'll choose to accept your responsibilities in something, and stop blaming everyone else.

I don't know how it pertains to you, but today, we are each urged to walk in peace for a specific reason.

I dreamed of spiders last night.

Beautiful red and gold spiders, so stunning they looked like jewelry.

I was wearing a long dress that brushed the ground, and I looked down and saw a spider at my feet. Then I moved away, and saw that there was another spider just like it on the hem of my dress.

I reached down to brush it off but it was stuck. So I got a stick and pried it off, and beneath it, were two more spiders, each on top of the other, and I had to pry each one to get it off.

One spider at my feet.

Three spiders on the hem of my dress.

The spider on the ground is the manuscript I just edited and sent back.

The first spider on the hem of my dress is the manuscript I am trying to finish that needs to be turned in.

The second spider is the manuscript with copy edits waiting to be edited.

The third spider is the book I have to write next that is due by the end of the year.

Their beauty represents the magic in my stories.

Their number signifies the tasks I have to complete relating to the stories.

Spiders represent many things in different cultures, but across the board, their presence signifies patience and creativity, and in my world, that speaks for itself.

Sent with peace.
    Sent with light.
    Sent with love.

A day stretches out before you. Blank pages as yet unwritten upon.

    How do **you** approach this day?

. . .

Spirit says:
>   Don't write on the pages in ink.
>   I take that to mean don't do or say things you can't take back.
>   Spirit says:
>   Don't make fiction out of truth.
>   I take that to mean don't lie to further your goals.
>   Spirit reminds you:
>   One day...each page you have written on will become your book.
>   Make it worthy of yourself.
>   Make it a memory worthy of leaving behind.

Sent with peace.
>   Sent with light.
>   Sent with love.

✿

I dreamed a book last night.
I've already made all the necessary notes, although I won't forget it, because in the dream, I was there.

The water pressure issue in my kitchen sink has FINALLY been fixed.

I hate living in a rental property, and depending on a leasing company for repairs. Before I lost myself, I took care of my own problems, and made my own decisions about my house. Now I live in someone else's house, and await their pleasure as to when or if things are going to be fixed.

But after having myself a fit with the leasing company, a real plumber was here this morning. Took him 5 minutes. 5 MINUTES....and he was done.

All the crap I put up with for three whole months, and all of the fixit men that leasing company sent first. The worst was the guy leaning over my sink watching a How-To on YouTube. When I saw him doing that, I told him, never mind, and sent him on his way. All the wasted money just because they went a cheaper route.

But I learned a long time ago that you get what you pay for.

It would best serve them in the long run to follow that practice.

I also learned the hard way that if you don't stand up for yourself and what's right, nothing is going to change.

When that water started flowing freely, after three months of a trickle, I felt like a wildcatter who had been drilling for oil, and finally struck pay dirt.

Only it's not oil to make me rich.

It's water. To drink. To clean with. To cook with. To wash my dishes with.

It's a small thing to fuss about until you don't have it available.

Then you get what all the fuss was about.

Happy day.

Spirit says:

The power of a word comes in the others used with it - and the manner and tone in which it is spoken.

You might not fully understand the scope, but you will feel the intention.

If you don't trust what's being said to you, or you don't trust the person saying it, then that is your soul warning you to beware of false promises, and false prophets.

Sent with peace.
    Sent with light.
    Sent with love.

ॐ

I have been in the saddest state for two straight days and couldn't figure out what was causing it until tonight as I was writing - and crying - as I've been doing for the past two days.

It's the story. I'm in a sad, sad, part of the story and when I write, I'm them...I'm the characters. I'm in the story. I'm there. And we're all sad, and we're all crying, and I got lost.

Lord. I know this is how I came, and I don't know any other way to be, but at least I've finally gotten past the sad part.

I need to shoot somebody now.

I need to drop someone off a cliff and rescue them.

I need action. LOL

God bless the characters in the next few chapters, because they already know what's coming.

I'm done with crying.

I'm gonna make a bad guy sorry, and amp up my hero and heroine's world.

That's what I'm gonna do.

I can't control my world, and I can't control theirs.

I'm just the storyteller - the voyeur into the world of word magic.

Still waiting for magic in mine.

Spirit says:

The hardest things you will ever do in your life are the right things.

Not the easiest.

Not the most popular.

Not the ones you like best.

But the right things.

Sent with peace.

Sent with light.
Sent with love.

※

Spirit says:
There is no 'but' to a truth.
Own what you've said.
Own what you've done.
Move on.

Winston Miller is staring at me from his bed in the living room. I dare not even crunch a piece of ice from my cup, or he will beg for some. That dog does love to eat ice.

Geenie Dog just plopped down beside him with her butt in his face. Geenie does not enjoy ice.

At least she's not staring at me, waiting for me to entertain her. I'm willing the both of them to go to sleep.

Believe it or not, I have work to do that does NOT involve barking.

I turned on Food Network for my background music today.

Ina Garten can talk to them while I work.

Aaaaah. Success! Her voice has put the both of them to sleep.

Being an adult has less to do with age, than it does the ability to accept responsibility.

When I was a little girl, I did what the adults in my world told me to do. I was learning.

As I grew older, I followed teachers instructions, and then the instructions and orders of the people I worked for.

By the time I was married, I was programmed to follow orders.

So I did.

It took over half my life time to realize I had given away my power. I didn't even know I had sovereignty over who I was, and what I could do.

But once realizing it, and then doing nothing about it, was on me.

I learned a thing, and then did not accept the responsibility of my birthright.

The price I paid for this knowledge was dear.

I gave up everything to save myself.

And then in later years, gave up everything again, to save someone else.

Choices.

Decisions.

Accepting responsibilities.

Being the adult.

Growing up.

Growing old.

Nobody said it would be easy.

But it is the path we all walk in this life.

Some figure it out.

Some don't.

It doesn't mean you failed.

You're always somewhere.

It's just that some destinations are easier than others.

Sent with peace.
    Sent with light.
    Sent with love.

IT'S CALLED LIFE

There are people who can, and people who won't.

There are people who eat, and people who don't.
There are ways to be kind, and ways to be cruel.
There are ways to behave and not act the fool.
There are times that are hard and so painful to feel
There are times that rend, and times that will heal.
There is life to be lived, with each breath that we take.
Until our life is taken by decisions we make.
Waste not a day, not an hour, not a minute.
Life is precious. Just live it. While you're still in it.
By Sharon Sala

Sent with peace.
    Sent with light.
    Sent with love.

Dear Walmart,
I ran errands this morning and you were one of them.
Fourteen registers, but only two active.
Stood in a line of 8 people waiting to be checked out.
All of us with white hair...while all kinds of employees hovered around the other customers using self-checkouts.
If you're so freaking scared someone is going to walk out without paying for something, then get your ass back to the registers and check us out.
That is all.

Spirit says:
When you put greed above justice, and accept lies above truth for self-gain, that path will extinguish the light within you.
Spirit says:
It is not God's business to keep you honest.

It is your responsibility.
Spirit says:
Betrayal of a trust is a physical pain.
Once broken it is never the same.
Words spoken have power.
Once they strike at the heart and the soul, the damage is done.
Don't be so full of yourself that you think you have the right to interpret and direct someone else's life.
Don't speak carelessly when you do not have all the facts.
You are no one's judge or jury.
Mind no business but your own.
I don't know if Spirit was through, but I am, so I'm going off to mind my own business now.
Making cookies, and writing stories.

Sent with peace.
    Sent with light.
    Sent with love.

In a dream, I'm sitting in a car looking out my windshield.
Can't go anywhere, just there.
A young woman with yellow skin suddenly jumps on the hood and sits there in a squat position, looking at me with such rage and hate that I can feel it.
She's sick...that's why she's yellow. Everyone is getting sick...and there's no cure.
She's going to kill me.

I get out of the car and say to her..."Do you know Mr. Mayhew?"
And the look of hate disappears from her face, replaced by one of fear.

People are gathering now. All of them in varying stages of illness, watching.

I've said a name that means something there.

And then my alarm went off, and now I'm awake.

I don't know where I was in that dream, but I WAS THERE...spirit walking. And I don't know what that name means, but in that dimension, it mattered.

I never know what all that means anymore, and it really doesn't matter. Because I live here, and no matter how many places my spirit walks when I sleep, I wind up back here.

Nothing has been solved.

Nothing has been changed for me in this world.

I will smudge myself before I go to sleep tonight.

I don't want to go back there.

It is a diseased and dying world.

I think maybe I was in the future of this one, or in a adjacent dimension.

I hope not, but time will reveal the truth.

૭ે

Spirit says:

How you were raised as a child is how you will be.

What you saw as a child is what you will do.

What you heard as a child is how you will speak.

If your childhood was hard, and you were abused and mistreated, it is up to you to move out of your past.

You can change for the better, but not until you see a better way, hear a better voice to use, and treat people better than the way others treated you.

Sent with peace.

Sent with light.
Sent with love.

※

Spirit says:
You won't always get what you pray for, but your prayer will be answered.

I think that's the part of the Universe that makes it so hard for people to keep the faith.

We pray for many things. Some are what we want, and some are what we need.

We're operating from the standpoint of being human, and where we are in this world, without any memory of what we came here to do, or an understanding that what we might be praying for, is counter-intuitive to what we 'have to have' to finish this journey.

If we came here to experience lack and need, to have a greater understanding of those who suffer - to grow the compassion within our souls, then that's going to impact what we receive, regardless of prayers to the contrary, because it's not what we need to walk the path.

That's what makes it so hard to believe.

And that's why it's so important that we do.

Spirit says:
As always, it is your choice.
You have free will. It's part of the promise with which you came...that and the soul contract you signed to pursue a specific path.

Maybe that path as a human was for learning how to control impulse decisions.

Maybe it's soul curiosity with no understanding of what's involved within being human.

All I know is that it's hard to live here when justice does not exist as it should.

When across-the-board prejudice controls such a large percentage of the population's decisions.

When you are an ancient soul who has existed within a Universe of love and understanding for as long as there was God, and you wind up here with all of the issues that come with being human, then sometimes, that faith is all you have to get you through it.

Just remember....
>God's faith has no color.
>God's faith has no prejudice.
>God's faith is all about love.

Sent with peace.
>Sent with light.
>Sent with love.

Spirit says:
>**Let go. Let go. Let go.**
>Whatever is troubling you, let go.
>Whatever you're holding onto from the past, let go.
>Whatever you're trying to control, let go.

Spirit says:
>Trust and believe.

Accept and proceed.

You aren't being punished. Even if it feels like it.

You're in a valley. Life is full of them. But you have to let go of the stuff down in the valley, before you have both hands free to climb out.

You want things to change?

Then stop doing the same things over and over.

You want to be right instead of better?

Then stop complaining about where you are, because you're choosing to be a victim, instead of changing for your well-being.

Write down one thing you are thankful for today.

Then think about it as you go through your day, remembering all of the people who make that possible for you.

Do this every day in the month of November up to Thanksgiving Day, and then read your list aloud to yourself on that day, and give thanks for the people who have blessed your life.

Being thankful is far more important than the food. Food will fill your stomach, but gratitude will feed your soul.

Sent with peace.
Sent with light.
Sent with love.

&

Even though I am well-read enough, and have traveled enough in my life to recognize and understand how differently we use words for reference, it all comes down to what part of the U.S. you come from.

Our points of reference for words and language in this nation is truly regional. They can be so different that you might as well have been born in another country.

The first time I went to New York City, I couldn't understand even half of what the people were saying. They spoke fast, and with different accents. The words they used to reference places and people, and the names they called their food were almost foreign to me. Yes, I knew the words, but they meant something different where I came from.

Some people make fun of others they call rednecks, or hillbillies, but that hill country language has been proven to be remnants of the language spoken from the first European settlers.

People also laugh at the slow, gentle, drawl of a southern voice.

And so it goes with all versions and dialects of the American English, which we know and accept, is different from the English of Great Britain.

And it occurs to me daily, that if we are that different in understanding each other, and we live in the same nation, no wonder there are people here who distrust people from other countries.

What you don't understand, you often fear, because you feel threatened by your inability to communicate.

It's hard to learn a second language.

I refuse to call it a foreign language because that separates us even more. Foreign has become a bad word, when all it means is unfamiliar...or from another place.

So, if I'm from Oklahoma and you're from Michigan, does that make me a foreigner in your state?

In the South, being from the North is still a thing. It goes all the way back to the Civil War.

Some people want us to be separate because of skin color, and try to sell the bullshit story that white people settled this country, therefore, anyone other than a white person is less than.

But if you are honest with yourself for even one second, you know that is a lie.

And they try to convince those ignorant of our history, that this country was founded on Christian religion, when it truth, the settlers were often people trying to escape religious persecution of all kinds in their native lands.

And yet look at what we've become - the very thing their ancestors were running from. The annihilation of people for their religious beliefs..

The People - First Nation people, were always here.

And their skin is brown. And it is beautiful.

And they speak a second language...it is called English.

Because their tribal languages are the first languages...just as they are the first people.

I tell you all this, because of Spirit's message today.

Spirit says:

What we ask of life is the same for all, even though it is asked for in different tongues.

If you judge another for being different from you, then you must accept you, too, are the foreigner in their world.

Sent with peace.
    Sent with light.
    Sent with love.

We will not be having a Thanksgiving dinner at my house this year. We're just having a meal, like any other day. No guests.

No hustle and bustle cooking.

Life, loss, and recent deaths, have given us a different perspective on what to be thankful for this year, and it's not a big meal.

So we let go of what was, to make room for what comes.

I had a dental appointment this morning.

It didn't hurt.

But I have a headache now.

I hurt myself by dreading it every time.

Stress is pain without the tears.

You weren't born onto this earth for your own pleasure and gain.

You didn't come here to make bad decisions.

You are a victim in your mind, only.

Tap into the power of the God-light within you.

The cord that exists between you and heaven is the ultimate charging station.

Be grateful for the chance to make a difference in the world.

Honor yourself.

Cherish you.

God loves you and so do I.

Sent with peace.

Sent with light.

Sent with love.

※

Spirit says:

You are the author of your life story.

You are the hero and the heroine.

The pacing and the drama.

The humor and the strife.
You are the love story, and the betrayal.
You create with free will.
Each day is a page.
Each life change becomes a new chapter.
Don't force the plot and pacing.
Your choices will take care of that.
And you, the author -
Will write the words -THE END.

Sent with peace.
    Sent with light.
    Sent with love.

ନ୍ତ

I'm not sleeping well at night and dozed off a little while ago.
    Dreamed I put myself up for adoption.
    I guess I'm through taking care of myself.
    But it was a bust. There were no takers.

Spirit says:
    Things are darkest because lights are out.
    You need light to see.
    You need to see to be able to change your point of view.
    To change your point of view, turn on a light.
    The one within you.
    Do for someone else.
    Be kind to someone else.
    Send prayers to someone else.
    Light burns brightest when you're giving, not receiving.

. . .

Sent with peace.
   Sent with light.
   Sent with love.

※

When I was a little girl, the first weekend after Thanksgiving would have been when my Grand made her fruitcakes.

She loved fruitcake, even the little candied citron bits that I found bitter. And because she loved them, and I loved her so much, I decided I loved fruitcake, too.

I can remember helping her measure out the raisins and the nuts, and the candied fruit bits. My favorites were the red and green candied cherries.

After the loaf cakes were baked and cooled, she would brush a sweet syrup made of water, sugar, and orange juice on them, and then wrap them in waxed paper, and then cheesecloth. Then once a week, she would unwrap them, brush them with more of the sugar syrup, and wrap them back up again, repeating it until Christmas.

By then, all those candied fruits, and that syrup, had soaked into the cake, turning it into a dark, sweet bite of fruit, and nut-filled, goodness.

But the things about 'helping' Grand do anything, were the life lessons. Things she talked about as we worked that I soaked up like a sponge.

Watching her and my Grampy being good to each other, how kind and considerate they were toward each other.

And the love was obvious. I never thought it strange to see people I viewed as 'old' still being in love. It seemed like how it was supposed to be.

Listening to her talk about what it was like to grow up in those times. Before statehood. Before women had the right to vote.

Listening to her tell about riding in the wagon with her Papa as he delivered the rural mail.

Teaching me how to crack and separate eggs without breaking the yolks. How to tell when you've kneaded yeast bread enough to set it to rising. Giving quick breads a light touch with little stirring, and no kneading. Measuring liquids with one kind of measuring cup, and flours and sugars with another.

I learned fractions from helping her cook, before I ever learned it in school. How many times to fill up a 1/2 cup measure to get 1 3/4 cups of sugar. Knowing that you can add vinegar to whole milk and substitute it in a recipe that calls for buttermilk.

The knowledge was ongoing, and endless.

So today, I am thinking of Grand, and wishing for one more time in the kitchen with her, measuring that candied citron, and the raisins and candied cherries, and listening to her fuss when Grampy stole a cherry out of the bowl. Catching the wink he gave her as went out the door, and seeing the little smile she tried to hide.

It was a good time in my world - being a child in that family.

I was blessed.

❧

Because I live in a city now, I check locks on doors a lot.
During the day.
Before I go to bed.
I never feel safe here.
But am I locking myself in? Or am I locking the world out?
One is an act of fear. The other is an act of rejection.

Spirit says:
Trusting without caution is rash.
Trust is a thing to be earned.

Once someone has proven they cannot be trusted,
And you still let them into your life, the fault is now yours.

Sent with peace.
   Sent with light.
   Sent with love.

*

When you fall on hard times, the false friends fall away.
   The family you can no longer help is suddenly absent.
   The silence is telling.
   And the people willing to tell you what you did wrong, are always the ones who need to tend to their own mess first.
   But by that time, you already know that your first mistake was trusting someone else's word, instead of trusting yourself.
   It's God's way of sorting through the chaff in your life.
   Hurtful. Sometimes shocking. But it is what it is.
   Be strong.
   If you want to be rescued, learn to swim.

Spirit says:
   Christmas is a human holiday.
   God's world is not about commerce.
   It's always joyful, giving, loving, sharing, and it costs nothing but faith.
   Live Christmas year 'round. Not just once a year.

Sent with peace.
   Sent with light.
   Sent with love.

Someone asked me the other day what I wanted for Christmas.
   I didn't know whether to laugh or cry.
   I not only don't want gifts.
   I don't want Christmas.
   But it's coming, so what I want is to be debt free, but that's not going to happen, either.
   So I'm not asking for anything because what I have is enough.
   I have my daughter and my grandson living with me.
   That is my gift.
   And it is enough.
   I am not on the streets.
   And that is enough.
   I have food.
   That is enough.
   I have a warm coat in a cold winter.
   That is enough.
   I have a car to drive.
   That is enough.
   It is all enough.

When I moved out of my house, I had to give away things that broke my heart. So there is nothing anyone can buy me now that will make that better.
   I don't want more of anything.
   I have enough.
   Spirit says:
   Be at peace with yourself.
   I'm working on that.

Sent with peace.
   Sent with light.

Sent with love.

❦

I have been spirit walking for the past two nights...

Once, it was me walking my own path, and I was given a message I'm still thinking about. And the other one, I am "in" someone else's viewpoint, which means it's not me there, but I'm witnessing it through her eyes.

The first dream was a message.

I am in a room full of people, and there are different tables set around the room, like banquet tables. People are milling around and I'm just there - like an observer. Someone comes up, hands me a high heel shoe that is made of faded flower fabric, and tells me to just pick a table and put the shoe on it.

I asked why, but she said, just pick a table, so I did.

And the moment I set the shoe on a table, the man who was standing behind it ran.

And then I turned around, and I'm no longer inside the room, and I'm watching two men digging a grave, and there's an open wooden coffin beside it.

I turn around and wake up.

I've never dreamed anything like this before, so I'm still thinking about it.

I did research it a bit, but there are dozens of different meanings, depending on which sites you use.

None of it pertains to Native American beliefs, because they didn't bury their dead like that, nor did they wear those kinds of shoes, but I know there's a message in it. Maybe I'll dream the answer later.

. . .

The other one happened the next night...and I KNOW I was witnessing human trafficking on a higher scale. And it wasn't me. I was seeing/experiencing it through someone else's eyes.

A young woman was at a gathering, just talking to people, when a handsome young man came up to her, told her he'd been watching her from across the room, and wanted to introduce himself because she was so charming. She smiles and falls for the line. He says he's going to get them each a glass of wine. She says..."no, thank you, I don't drink," but he ignores her, saying that's ridiculous, and brings back the drink.

She holds it, but doesn't taste it. So then he pulls out a stunning, one of a kind bracelet, and wraps it around her wrist. The stones are pale blues and greens, in settings meant to reflect forget-me-nots (the flowers). She tries to take the bracelet off, but it won't come off, so she slips away into another room, and then some tall stern-faced woman approaches her, and tells her she's not supposed to leave, and I'm feeling that young woman's panic when I wake up.

These dreams are exhausting. I'm supposed to be resting at night and instead, this is happening. Spirit asks a lot of me all the time. And I give, and I give of myself, because that is my path, but I'm about to call a halt here. Spirit is using me up. But nothing is being refilled.

That's when I have to take control of what I am willing to receive, and what I'm willing to do.

You might wonder why I tell you all this. But I feel like there are others like me out there who don't understand why they are how they are, and they don't understand that what they're dreaming doesn't always apply to them. That they are like radio stations. Receivers of messages. And sometimes when we're not paying attention, we receive messages meant for other people, too. It's not our responsibility to deliver them. So don't freak out about it.

Just think of it like walking into a spider web. You didn't know it was there. You didn't see it coming. But it felt weird, and left you kind of in a panic that the spider in that web was now on you.

Only in these instances, the spider in that web you walked into doesn't see you and isn't looking for you. You just walked into someone else's dream.

Sent with peace.
   Sent with light.
   Sent with love.

***

Yesterday, everyone was talking about the anniversary of the bombing of Pearl Harbor in 1941, which was when the U.S. joined the allies in fighting WWII.

I was born in 1943. My soul came to Earth in the middle of a war. I was but one of tens of thousands of souls who were born between the years of 1939 and 1945, which was the duration of WWII...

We were born into hardship and sadness. And some of those babies, who were born where the war was being fought, knew the sounds of air raid sirens, before they ever heard their mothers sing a lullaby.

Here in the U.S., everything went to the military first.

Rubber was rationed, so tires were at a premium. Sugar was rationed, as was coffee...fuel...even women's nylon stockings, because the nylon was being used first for parachutes. Anything that was being used in the war became scare here, and America rationed out what was left to the population.

. . .

I grew up hearing the whispers of families getting the news that their people who had gone to war had died. I remember hearing the women in my mother's family crying about the death of one of our own.

Like so many others, my childhood was laced with war, and stories of war.

I barely remember the years when we have been at peace here.

This is not a unique story, by any means, and we have been at war almost non-stop on this earth since the existence of humanity. So why do I mention this?

Because Spirits says:
    War has never solved anything.
    Killing has never proved a point.
    Dying is an end to the possibility of change.
    Spirit says:
    Those who provoke war, do it for gain.
    Those who die in war, are sacrifices for someone else's greed.
    Those who live by the sword, die by the sword.
    And just for the record, I didn't really want to post this.
    But Spirit directs me, and so I do as I am led.
    I suppose this will speak to some, and anger others.
    And that is your right.
    I didn't write this for a pat on the back.
    I didn't post it expecting people to agree.
    I simply delivered a message from Spirit.
    You either receive it, or you don't.
    Proceed with your day.

Spirit says:

It is an ignorance of the past that leads youth to repeat it in the future.

This is a powerful message that is never going to reach the ones in need - because the majority under the age of thirty don't read content anymore. They have the attention spans of gnats. Their focus lasts through three or four sentences of snark on social media, which is sent and read it in illiterate text. But I delivered it anyway.

And that's the path they chose. Being led by others through mindless entertainment.

They don't know and don't care that, by giving up truth and knowledge, they are giving up control of their own lives. That they are creating a future where, but a few, control the masses.

We're already almost there.

I hope I die before I see this happen. But it is their choice. Their own free will to choose to be less than - and it is where they'll be.

Yesterday I saw something rare for this part of the state...an eagle flew over my house. I was driving up my street when I saw it fly over my house. I stopped and watched it soaring above me, dipping and circling, turning and then soaring upward and away. The size of it, and the white feathers alone were impossible to mistake.

It was a message from Bobby.

His Native name was Lvmhe, which means eagle, in the Muscokee language.

He knows how heartsick I am about what's happened to my life, and what I've lost, and how uprooted I feel. He knows how much I miss him. The eagle was beautiful to see, but it does not change my fate.

All it says to me is that he loves me.

I don't exactly know why this is all happening to me, but life has officially broken me.

I asked Spirit for help, when what I needed was a miracle.

I got neither, and I'm still here.

It is what it is.

※

Spirit says:

That which you acknowledge, you bring to you.

Good or bad, you have issued the invitation.

I think I've always known this on a subconscious level, and then Bobby reminded me a long time ago that speaking words gives them power.

That which you speak, you give life to.

So I never acknowledge the dark ones by name.

I don't talk about them.

I don't wish them on people.

I don't make jokes about them.

They aren't allowed to come into this dimension without invitation. But we all know many do speak of them and invite them, so they are everywhere. Just not in my house - not in my world.

I don't watch horror. I don't read it. I don't speak it.

I don't let that into my life.

Spirit said it... And so it is.

Sent with peace.
    Sent with light.
    Sent with love.

※

The time to act on whatever you've been dreaming about is always now.

Waiting for the perfect moment will never come, because life isn't perfect.

It wasn't meant to be.

But it is meant to be experienced to the fullest - from the darkest parts of it, to the brightest heights of it.

Spirit says:

Love is everything.

I believe that. I have always believed love mattered most. Part of that is what got me where I am. Loving everyone more than I loved myself.

That's the trick about being whole. You really need to love yourself, too.

Today I begin another chapter in the Blessings book I'm working on. It seems fitting to be writing about my fictional town of Blessings again, in the midst of all the blessings of prayers I've been sent, and money donated to help me through this hard time. It won't fix my financial situation, but it is the emotional uplift I needed.

It is the season for blessings, they say.

But in my town of Blessings, the spirit of giving, and loving, is year-round. Maybe that's why I love writing about it so much.

Because it's how I think the world should be.

People helping each other.

Lifting each other up in times of hardship and sadness.

Miracles happening. Small ones. Surprising ones. Knocking your socks-off-amazing ones.

That's why I love writing about the little town of Blessings, Georgia. If it was an actual place, I would be living there.

But it does exist in my heart, and in my mind, and so when I write the stories of Blessings, I'm writing them for you, as well as for me, because everyone should know what being loved, and accepted, is all about.

Spirit says:
You are never closer to God than when you are taking care of someone else, and doing it from a place of love.

Sent with peace.
 Sent with light.
 Sent with love.

※

Spirit says:
If EVERYONE in the world thought (at the same time) about healing everyone who was sick, it would happen.
That much love and energy, focused for the same reason, at the same instant, would put so much power into the Universe it would be blinding.
It's what we're capable of doing. But it will never happen the way people are now, because hate is stronger than love.
Prejudice is stronger than acceptance.
Exclusion is stronger than belonging.

So we suffer, and we fall ill, and we grieve, and we wonder why our hearts don't heal, and why we can't find our joy, and why the world is always at war.
The dark ones make sure we are always at odds.
And we're so conditioned to being told what to do, and when to do it, that we blindly follow without proof that it is the good thing, or the right thing, or the fair thing, or the loving thing.
Spirit asks:

But now that you know.... Will you care?

Sent with peace.
   Sent with light.
   Sent with love.

                                                                   ❧

The details of a life are in the decor.

We all have ideas of what makes us comfortable, and what we think is pretty.

We're also limited financially by what we can afford to add to our life in the way of comfort.

But it costs nothing to put joy in your home.

Laughter is free.

Love is innate.

When a house is full of beauty, but every emotion in it is negative, then it is not a home.

Putting a positive spin on the worst day of your life isn't easy, but it's possible. Finding one bright spot on which to focus, is how you move through it - knowing you are not alone in your suffering.

You can't buy your way out of grief.

You can't own enough to make yourself happy if you hate how you feel.

Yes, money would solve the problems that may be the cause of your stress.

But it won't cure the rage in your heart - or the jealousy you live with - or the prejudice with which you move through your day - or the ugliness of your constant judgment of others.

For the time we are on earth, our soul inhabits our body. It is our soul's home away from home. When we let that home be fouled with negativity, and we abuse that body in any way, we are destroying the home our soul inhabits.

A soul/spirit never dies, but sometimes we are so toxic by the time we are released from this earthly plane, that we go home sick. Even a bit broken. And have to spend time healing from what has happened to us here.

If you care about how the dwelling you live in looks.

And you care about the physical appearance you present to the world.

Then you should also care about the inner you, as well.

Sent with peace.
    Sent with light.
    Sent with love.

I have never in my life wanted to go back in time, but I do now.

I want my childhood back.

I didn't know how precious it was then, or how fleeting it would be.

I didn't know the people you loved wouldn't live forever.

If I had, I would have hugged them more, laughed more, played more, loved harder.

I didn't know how fast some would disappear.

I didn't know that you could lose someone, years before their actual death.

When I was a child, I went to bed each night snuggled up beside my sister, and woke up knowing mother and daddy were in the kitchen, preparing for the day.

That was my security, knowing I was loved within that circle.

I didn't know being an adult would be so hard, or so sad.

The irony of my adult life is that it's nothing I ever planned.

Being a writer was nothing I even dreamed of.

And yet it was my destiny.

That much I know for sure.

I know everything I've learned in life is imbued within the words I write. How could it not be?

The way we see the world is how a story evolves.

I often write stories with dark storylines, but the thread of light, and love, and hope, is always there.

It's part of my path. To plant the seeds of hope where none has grown.

But I could never write something that offends me personally.

I would never write something that offends me morally.

It would poison the well within me.

It is not a judgment against others.

It is just MY truth.

To keep alive the stories within me, I have to be true to myself.

And I accept the financial hardship that comes by not following a trend.

I treasure the readers who've stayed with me.

I am so grateful for all of you who have helped me financially, in the past few weeks.

And for the friends I have gathered along the way, who have stepped into the empty places in my heart, that came from losing family. I know I can't have my childhood back, but I am so grateful for you.

Sent with peace.
   Sent with light.
   Sent with love.

MY DAY BEFORE CHRISTMAS STORY

I was in Walmart yesterday morning, and it seemed that every aisle I went up or down, I kept meeting the same elderly woman, with the same couple right beside her, who were helping her shop.

Once upon a time, I think she was tall, but life had put a stoop in her shoulders, and bent her back near in half. She was leaned over, and hanging onto the cart as she walked, and every time we met in an aisle, we smiled at each other in passing.

I think it was the kinship of two gray-haired ladies hanging onto shopping carts to keep from face-planting in the aisles that made the connection, but by the fifth time it happened, she just flat-out grinned at me.

I stopped, laughed, and patted her arm and said..."From the looks of your cart,(which was filling up, while mine had only three items in it) I think I need to have Christmas with you."

And the first words out of her mouth were..."You just come on down! We'd love to have you."

It was all I could do not to hug her right where we stood, but we smiled, and then moved along. I didn't see her again, but today she's still in my heart.

This was how my world used to be. This was how people were when I was a little girl. Open, genuine in their welcome, and honest in the invitation.

This was how my Grand received drop-in neighbors who had a propensity for showing up unannounced right at noon dinner, or at the evening supper.

They were greeted with joy at the door and the kids sent outside to play. Grampy was sent to the basement to get another quart of green beans, and Grand began peeling an extra two or three more potatoes to slice up in the skillet, and added a few more strips of their home-cured bacon to fry.

I've been witness to that. I've been a part of that. The common ground of sharing what they had was a given.

I felt blessed yesterday by that moment with the woman...

I was reminded then, of my favorite bible verse...Hebrews 13:2

"Be not forgetful to entertain strangers: for thereby ye may have entertained angels unawares."

That elderly woman was my angel - the messenger sent for me yesterday, on that hard day at the tax lawyer's office later - to remind me that while all may seem lost - love is not.

Sent with peace.
 Sent with light.
 Sent with love.

Spirit says:
 Anger and resentment often hold you back from fulfilling your soul contract.
 Forgiveness matters.
 Going forward often means letting go of the old things. The sad things. The dark things. Anything that anchors you to that.

Spirit says:
 A new day is a new beginning.
 A new year is a spiritual push to move forward.
 And so it is.

Sent with peace.
 Sent with light.
 Sent with love.

It's raining here today.
 Dreary...chilly...one of those kind of days.
 I'm still writing on another Blessings book.
 In the book, it's just after New Years Day, and in reality, we

haven't had New Year's Day yet. So my real time, and my inner timeline, aren't quite synced.

Wish I was finished with the book, but I'm not.

Somebody asked me the other day if I could travel anywhere, where would I go.

I replied. "Off this planet."

That's my chosen destination.

I just put a pecan pie in the oven.

Kathy is making a cheese ball of some kind.

I went to the mall yesterday and bought a little Hickory Farms Beef stick (it's all 50% off).

My son and family are coming to eat lunch with us tomorrow.

Looking forward to that.

Hope the weather is better.

We're having baked ham left from our Christmas dinner, and making chicken and rice, green beans, and coleslaw. Kathy's making a cheese ball and little tidbits of the Summer Sausage beef stick with crackers, olives, etc.

I think ya'll call that a charcuterie board.

We call it snacks.

I didn't know how to pronounce charcuterie, and I didn't know how to spell it. Had to look it up. But that's okay. I know it exists. I know what it means. And now I know how to spell and pronounce it.

But it will not be used in my daily vocabulary any time in the near future, so I'm good.

Spirit says:

The price of ignorance is high.

You can fall for anything if you don't know the difference.

Ignorance is not bliss.

It is dangerous.

. . .

Sent with peace.
   Sent with light.
   Sent with love.

Spirit says:
The way you live is due to the choices you make.
   The level of knowledge you have, comes from your exposure to learning new things.
   The composite of you, is derived from all you have experienced, and survived.
   But if you are continuing to make the same choices, and then are frustrated with the same results, you have learned nothing from your life experiences.
   You aren't applying what you've learned to your future.
   However, this is your choice to make.
   If you don't like where you are, make different choices.
   I feel like Spirit has been sending this message for some time now.
   But as always, I just repeat what I'm meant to deliver.
   Evidently, the word isn't being received or I wouldn't be getting this in such a way.
   I guess it's like a parent constantly telling their child, stop putting that bean up your nose, as they're taking them to ER for the fifth time to get it out - and the kid is bawling all the way.
   Someone hasn't learned to stop putting the bean up their nose.
   So, going into a new year, it appears the message is about making new choices. Not old ones. And trying not to repeat our same mistakes.
   Sent with peace.
   Sent with light.
   Sent with love.

Spirit says:
   You know what.
   You know how.
   You know change that you desire begins and ends with YOU.

Spirit says:
   All that you desire is not always what you need.
   Need should always come before greed.
   But greed often precedes the wise choices.
   Think of consequences before you proceed.

Traditions are part of our lives.
   Some traditions are meaningful to people.
   Others have just become habit without remembering the reason.
   For as long as I can remember, my people, me included, have always cooked and eaten black-eyed peas on New Year's Day. It's supposed to be for good luck.
   I ate them religiously, because I was afraid not to.
   I'm not the kind who ever wanted to dare fate.
   But at my age, and having eaten black-eyed peas every January 1st, for at least seventy-three of my seventy-six years of living, I can state with total assurance that the only thing you will receive from eating black-eyed peas is gas.
   Luck does not ensue, because there is no such thing as luck.
   You receive blessings, but you don't get lucky.
   Luck is just another word for random chance.
   Do not bet your life - your hopes - your future - on the random chance of so-called luck.
   And, having come to this conclusion, after the past fifteen years of hell I have endured - and the consequences that came with it - those peas do not work.
   So, I'm breaking tradition this year.

In the year of our Lord, 2020, I am not eating black-eyed peas today.

But I am moving forward. And I am changing directions.

I want to be happy again.

And the only person who can change how I feel is me.

I'm sending resolutions for your troubles.

I'm sending love, light, and peace into the Universe to be showered upon you.

I'm sending white healing light for good health for you.

I'm sending understanding to you.

I'm sending wisdom that you see the truth of what has kept you lost.

I'm sending peace to your troubled life.

I'm sending light to the dark places within you.

I'm sending love, because in The Universe that is God...it is worth more than gold.

Spirit says:
There are no rules to starting over.

One day you just get enough, and stop doing everything the same old way, and change your mind.

Change is good.

It's growth.

One day you look in a mirror - past the hair spray and the makeup - past the lines you're trying to hide - past the vanity that guides you to spending money on products to disguise who you really are.

You look at your eyes, and then look into your own eyes.

And you stare.

Because you don't recognize that woman anymore.

She'd not what you planned to be at this age.

She doesn't look how you thought you looked.
But she's better.
That woman is real.
Rather than being disappointed, or disapproving of her, you should get to know this woman.
She is the culmination of all your life choices.
She is who's still standing after crisis and grief.
She is who stood in the gap for loved ones when no one else would.
She's the one who took jobs for less than she was worth without complaining, because sacrifice is what people do in the name of love.
Sure, she made mistakes, but everyone makes mistakes.
Not repeating them is the key.
The Change Your Life Train is always running.
You don't need a ticket.
You just get on board.

Sent with peace.
Sent with light.
Sent with love.

If there was a kiosk in our local mall that sold Macarons like the one in Penn Square Mall in Oklahoma City, I would so be there today.

They are my go-to sugar fix for my sad. What I eat to shift my anger - to re-route my focus - and a general, all-around good thing to eat.

Hell on my blood sugar. But we've all got to die some day, right?

Some cupcake place here in the city used to sell them, but if I'm gonna mainline sugar, I want the good stuff. Otherwise, I'll just mope.

. . .

Today I'm sending out love to everyone who's dealing with grief.
However you're feeling it...no matter how old, or how fresh.
I don't need to know your story.
You just need to know I'm sending love.
I don't want to read about what caused it.
I just want you to know you aren't suffering it alone.
So many people in distress.
So many people in crisis.
Too many people looking away.
Too many of us helpless to change the world.
Prayer's not going to do it because there's not enough people praying for it.
They say it takes a village to raise a child...
But it takes all of humanity. All of us. To change the world.
We talk about it.
We argue about it.
We pray about it.
And then it goes out of our thoughts until the next atrocity, or the next affront.
Then we start all over, pointing fingers, calling names, blaming each other, and nothing changes.
But I won't forget you.
I'm still praying for your hearts to ease.
For you to find your place of peace within your grief.
I can't send you Macarons. But I send you love.

Sent with peace.
Sent with light.
Sent with love.

Spirit says:

It's hard to rationalize justice when it's not the same for everyone.

But that all comes from the laws of man, not from God.

It is a sin against humanity that health care is sorted out by who can pay, and who cannot. It's like saying those with money matter, and those without do not.

Humanity has created its own worst nightmare.

Partitioning people off like cattle. Sorting them by financial status. Then by religion. Then by race. And finally, by the color of their skin.

I dreamed last night that the United States of America no longer existed. That Russian soldiers were in the streets, ordering people out of houses, rounding them up like cattle.

Our technology had been turned off. Banks that held our money now belonged to communist Russia. And the money had been confiscated by the government.

I dreamed that I was standing in the street in front of a house - my house. Soldiers were pointing guns at me, shouting at me. Ordering me to get in the truck. But I just stood there. And so did the other people in the other houses. We'd already decided we would not comply.

Earthquakes were happening in the world in record numbers, and everything was on fire. Volcanoes were erupting.

And we'd already decided what was left of the world was not worth fighting for.

A soldier pointed a gun at me again, and I turned around to face the house, said a prayer to the Old Ones that I had not forgotten the injustices of the past, then aimed the remote I was holding and pressed a button.

The house exploded, and I was gone - but so were they.

And all along the streets, the other people were doing the same thing.

We knew they were taking us to death camps.

So we chose our own way to die, and took them with us.

And then I woke up.

I'm not saying that was a premonition.

But I know that I would do that before I'd ever bow down.

It was a dream. Just a dream.

But in the dream, I fought back. My way.

I died on my terms. In my country.

And like the warriors of my People - I took the enemy with me.

It was a vivid dream. I'm still processing it.

It's nothing that foretells your future. It's all mine.

All it meant - at least to me - is that my life happens on my terms.

Not by the death of other people. But death to a way of life.

Not by killing people. Just ending dreams.

That's how my dreams work. They are analogies for other things.

Now, imagine you're me.

This was what you slept with last night, and today you have to go to another place inside your head, and write more on the book you're working on. The book that's set in the place where everything always ends happy ever after.

Your old world is already dying.

You don't know where you'll be six months from now.

But you, by God, still know how to escape it.

You write about where you want to be, and the people you wish to live with - and do everything you can to finish out this life with as much dignity and grace as the Good Lord will allow.

. . .

Sent with peace.
Sent with light.
Sent with love.

&.

Spirit says:

When you speak, whatever words you are saying are given life.

Once you have given life to words, you gave them power.

Power put into action without thought, has the same consequences as a lit match thrown into kindling.

It will burn.

Spirit says:

Gossip is the same thing as a lie. You have no way of knowing if what you were told was the truth, but you're spreading it anyway. So you participate in a lie.

And then you judge.

And the damage is done.

One of the directives in a doctor's oath is "First, do no harm."

That should be the initial thought in everyone's mind before they speak, or before they act.

But it's not.

Right now - in this world, in this time, our first action is anger, our second is rage. And the next thing that happens is violence.

After that come the outcries of injustice, and beyond that, the people who offer to pray it away, which is actually taking the easy way out. Because all you're doing is dumping it in God's lap, and begging him to fix the mess that was made.

The thing about being human is that you agreed to it before you came. You also knew that the free will you were given, and the choices you made, would be on you.

You don't bother God with your good days.

But you drop to your knees on the bad days.

Always. Every day. Thank God.

Some days you thank Him for the good day.

Some days you thank Him for strength to get through the bad ones.

When you speak, the tone of your voice, and the words you use to make known a request, or a need, or a dissatisfaction, do not need to be assaults just to make yourself heard.

You have to be quiet to hear your own conscience.

And you need to be listening.

It is the voice of God speaking to you.

Sent with peace.
>   Sent with light.
>   Sent with love.

Spirit says:

Do not feed yourself lies because you are feeling sorry for yourself.

You cannot be replaced.

You are unique to this world, and your presence matters.

Wilma Mankiller, a past principal chief of the Cherokee Tribe of Oklahoma, once said..."If you have but one drop of Native blood, you are still part of the whole."

She was referring to people with Native blood who do not have enough to qualify them for tribal membership, even though their ancestry is Native.

But it is true of humanity, as well.

Your soul is as that drop of blood. It is part of the sum of human energy that creates the God-light upon this Earth, and when one soul goes missing here, even though another soul arrives - it does not fill the space in the same way - or with the same energy and

light.
>Never let someone tell you that you don't matter.
>Believe in yourself, because God believes in you.

Sent with peace.
>Sent with light.
>Sent with love.

☙

Last night in my dream...I was a scarecrow in the vast landscape of an empty field.

Crows were everywhere. Pecking at my button eyes. Pecking at my straw hair. Pecking at the buttons on my shirt.

There was no crop. No food. No produce. Just the scarecrow and the crows.

I had no mouth, so I had no voice.

The sky was black with crows when I woke up.

Just more analogies...it's a fear-based dream, and the fear is real.

I still have no resolutions.

I hate uncertainty.

Promises aren't reality.

Predictions are just guesses, subject to change.

I don't assume anything. Not anymore.

Life taught me this, and I'm a fast learner.

Today I'm writing again.

I trust me.

I trust my gift.

God gave it to me.

I trust God.

But since I can't hear Him, all I KNOW is that this is my time in the shadows. I alternate between angry, and sad.

Angry that it's happening again.

I've lost count of how many times this has happened to me in my seventy-six years.

Sad that it's happening again - in my seventy-sixth year.

But age is just a number.

It means nothing in the Universe.

It is but a blink of an eye...no longer than a thought.

Here, when things are good, they fly past too quickly to appreciate.

And when times are hard, they feel like an eternity.

It's just life.

And like it or not, at this time in my world, it is mine.

Spirit says:

"Oh ye of little faith, be at peace. You are not alone. You are not forgotten."

I received this message, and I have to be at peace with it. It's not the certainty I desire. It's not a real answer. But it is a message. So I share it with you, because that is my path.

Sent with peace.
   Sent with light.
   Sent with love.

❧

Spirit says: Write this. And so I do.
   Once upon a time in America....

Will be the title of someone's article. Or someone's book. And when they begin relating what we once were, and what we let happen, and what we'd done, and what we let slide that we didn't want to face, and what we tolerated because it did not affect us personally, and on, and on, and on, until the end of the article comes to what we became - it will be a tragedy of criminal errors unlike anything the world has ever seen.

. . .

Some will say it is preposterous. An elaborate hoax. A work of apocalyptic fiction, written with just enough pathos, to make it a best-seller.

That it can't really be true.

They won't understand the ennui of an entire country that led them to that end. They will not be able to believe how so few could destroy so many. They will not understand the masses who were blinded to truth, or be able to comprehend those people who fed upon the lies, and hid the truth within the waste of bodies, and lives, they left behind.

Once Upon a Time In America...

We thought we were great, but we weren't. Not really. The only people who believed that wholly, were white. We wanted to be great. But we stood upon the heritage of others we judged as lesser, and buried the bodies of those who witnessed our shame, in unmarked graves.

And so here we are.

Some call it karma.

Some call it the end of times.

But whatever it is. Whatever is left of us when this is over, needs to be better than what we were.

Sent with peace.
   Sent with light.
   Sent with love.

Spirit says:

No child comes into this world with the perception of prejudice.

That is a learned behavior.

Spirit in its purest form, before it reincarnates into a human body, is nothing but pure love and light.

It is only here on this earth - into whatever environment it has chosen to be born - that it encounters the heights and depths of what it means to be human - and learns what it came here to learn.

Spirit says:

This is something to remember - to help each of us understand why we are so different, and in constant fear of things we do not understand.

It's because where we came from was so perfect and so beautiful, that the transition from there, to here, can be more than some souls are able to bear.

The hate and anger are painful to them.

The confusion and inhumanity to one another is a foreign concept they do not understand.

In these instances, two things may happen.

They will either retreat from this world as introverts, unwilling to participate in society as it exists.

Or, they will succumb to the temptations of being human, and take the easy way out of strife, by hurting others to please themselves.

Only the strongest and the oldest of souls will prevail in times of trouble.

They become the voices of reason.

The people we could count on.

The ones who teach.

The ones who heal.

The ones who understand that when many souls focus all of their energy on one purpose at the same time, change will come.

Humans are selfish and self-centered.

Souls are not.

But at the birth of each child on this earth, one has been incorporated into the other.

And it will be environment that tenders the outcome of that single precious life.

Don't teach your child prejudice.

Don't show your child hate.

Don't damage the perfection of that which you were given, and then wonder what went wrong.

Sent with peace.
Sent with light.
Sent with love.

THIS IS HAPPENING

Australia on fire.

Earthquakes in Puerto Rico.

Volcanic Eruption in the Philippines.

Soldiers sent to another war.

Babies stolen from their parents.

Children in concentration camps in our country.

Human trafficking.

Crime and graft rampant in our government.

Lack of health care.

The random acts of mass shootings.

THE WORLD IS IN CRISIS, AND THIS IS WHAT YOU FIGHT ABOUT

Religion.

Megan and Harry (British royals who have nothing to do with America) decided to move to Canada.

Making fun of an autistic child who is fighting global warming.

Demeaning people who don't dress to please you.

Using Social Media to hurt others, because you're too big of a coward to say it to their faces.

What no one understands is, that the things happening in the first list, trigger what is done in the second list.

BECAUSE:

We feel helpless to put out a fire halfway across the world.

We cannot stop earthquakes.

We cannot prevent volcanic eruptions.

We have no power to stop a war.

We watch our loved ones dying from lack of health care.

We see our children go missing due to human trafficking.

We abhor what is happening to the children in concentration camps, but we have no power to change it.

The end result is:

Helplessness triggers anger.

Fear triggers rage and depression.

And our first reaction is to hurt someone else like we're hurting?

We're supposed to be adults.

What's wrong with this picture?

&

All my life, when I first wake up in the morning, I roll over on my back, but I don't open my eyes. I just lie there, waiting.

Sometimes I see a vision.

Sometimes I get messages.

Sometimes what I see, I know I'm never going to share.

People aren't always ready to hear a truth.

They're having so much trouble dealing with the reality of their life as it is, that taking on another revelation only makes things worse for them.

I don't consider it my job to stir the pot.

I am a Lightworker.

All that means is that, here on this earth, at this time, my job is to love, to be a peacemaker, to do no harm, and to live within The Word.

Love one another, as I have loved you.

Do unto others, as you would have them do unto you.

I am a messenger.

All that means is that I deliver messages.

That my messages come from Spirit bothers some people.

They might ignore it, considering me a crackpot.

They might make fun of it, calling me crazy.

They might feel the truth of it and strike out in anger because they see themselves in the messages.

None of that bothers me.

Because I did not create the message.

It did not come from me.

But it does come through me.

I deliver what I am told.

The rest of how it makes others feel is on them.

Proceed or ignore.

It matters not to me.

So this morning when I opened up to Spirit, there were no words. Only an overwhelming feeling of love pouring through me, and what I can only describe as empathy.

Empathy for you. For me. For humanity.

Love for all of us.

Spirit knows our sadness. But we created it.

Spirit sends messages, and warnings, and signs, all the time. But either we don't recognize them, or we ignore them.

Spirit loves us. But when that love doesn't change our circumstance, we reject it.

It's like a parent who loves their child so very much that they would die for them, and then has to watch that child create chaos for him/herself and others, without the power to change or stop them.

Like it or not. Agree with this or not.

That's where we are.

Sent with peace.
    Sent with light.
    Sent with love.

Spirit says:

A day will come when you have to stop following a herd, and follow your heart, instead.

Spirit says:

Standing alone can be sign of distinction.

Or it can be a sign of disagreement.

Either way, there is dignity in holding fast to what your heart says is right.

Sent with peace.
    Sent with light.
    Sent with love.

Spirit says:

When it's soul-felt, love is forever.

When it's fed purely from lust or passion, it is ephemeral. It comes into your life when you wanted it, and it leaves when you finally let it go.

When you understand that it was something you weren't meant

to keep, the acceptance of this truth is part of how a person moves forward in life.

Holding on to what no longer serves you becomes an anchor.

It will weaken the part of you that is meant to thrive.

You are giving so much of your time and energy into trying to make someone love you, that you don't nurture the rest of your life.

Or, you might be on the other end of that spectrum, and feel trapped in a relationship you know is detrimental to your personal happiness, but you either don't know how to let go, or you're afraid of the consequences if you do.

Love is powerful.

But obsession is the antithesis of love.

Obsession has boundaries.

Love for one another has none.

When someone you think you love begins isolating you from everything, and everyone else who is a part of your world, that isn't love.

That's your first sign of danger.

Making excuses to yourself for why you're letting it happen, is your first big mistake.

Always proceed with caution.

Love isn't love unless it's given freely.

Love isn't love unless it's received in the same way.

Spirit says:

Abide within your own heart until you find someone worthy of receiving it.

Sent with peace.

Sent with light.

Sent with love.

Spirit says:

Being part of a herd means you are being led by someone else's desires and wishes.

Spirit says:

Sheep who follow a wolf will get eaten.

Sent with peace.
    Sent with light.
    Sent with love.

🐾

Spirit says:

How you speak of others, is a direct reflection of what you think about yourself.

Think about that.

If you are constantly critical of other people.

If you talk snark on a daily basis about what other people are doing, how they look, etc., Spirit says it is subconscious reflection of what you think about yourself.

SO.

The next time I see the usual people on social media being all hateful and snarky about someone's looks again, or what someone else is doing that they don't like, or someone they feel the need to put down, I'm going to say a prayer for them, because they must hate themselves from the inside out, and that's no way to walk in this world.

Be at peace, ya'll.

If you don't love yourselves, I'm sending you some.

Every day I'll be saying a prayer for your heart to settle, and for the hateful words to taste bitter on your tongue, so that you will be reminded of what you are doing TO YOURSELF.

. . .

Sent with peace.
Sent with light.
Sent with love.

&.

I have been awake since 3:30 a.m., because my toilet began to leak around the base last night.

A nice slow leak, soaking up towels and bath mats.

But I no longer live in a house that is mine. So I am dealing with a leasing company via email ONLY, to let them know this development, while knowing they are closed for two days (they don't work on weekends) and will not see my message until Monday.

AT WHICH TIME I will have already dealt with the freaking leak myself, at my expense, because I am not going to wade water, waiting three days for a long-distance landlord's leasing company to respond.

(insert your own choice of curse words here. I used mine)

ONE STEP FORWARD.

TWO STEPS BACK.

But while I was lying there wondering how long it would take for the water to get to the carpet in the bedroom, Spirit butted in to let me know I wasn't awake alone.

Spirit is good like that.

Only Spirit's observation (I call it that, because this isn't a message) wasn't any more uplifting than my soggy bath mats.

Spirit said to me:

The saddest part of America right now is that we chose sides.

AGAINST EACH OTHER.

Balance is what makes things work.

We don't work right now because we are out of balance.

And that was Spirit's bit of wisdom to me in the wee damp hours of my morning. It wasn't uplifting. It didn't make me feel better, but then Spirit is not a cheerleader.

Spirit is conscience...wisdom...God light...Love....SO MUCH LOVE.

Spirit's voice is often the thing we know, but don't always want to accept.

When I was growing up, both political parties worked together to form a cohesive and strong government for our country.

The U.S. is broken.

There is no US anymore.

Only WE or THEM.

Sent with peace.
Sent with light.
Sent with love.

※

You never know when the Universe is asking you to perform a blessing. And even then, do you recognize the significance after it happens?

I do.

I always see it as it's happening, and am thankful I was trusted to fulfill the task.

Tonight, both Scout and I played a part in a stranger's blessing, and I want to share that with you.

My daughter came home from the store with packages of veggie tortellini to cook for supper tonight. On any other night, Scout wouldn't have thought twice about the menu, because he's ALWAYS happy with whatever is being made.

But tonight, he looked, and then asked his mom, "What is the meat that goes with it?" And she said, "There's not any. I'm sorry."

He just said that was okay, he'd figure something out.

I overheard, then because I wanted to help, I thought about KFC which is just down the street from where we live.

I told him, I'll go get you some chicken. Do you want chicken tenders or pieces, and extra-crispy or original?

He said crispy pieces, please, and off I went.

So I'm in the drive-thru line, and I see a homeless man standing at the corner, flat against the building beneath the shallow overhang. I see he's talking as cars are passing by him, but without heeding him.

When I drive up to where he's at, he asks, "Ma'am, I'm not asking for money. But I've been on the streets for five weeks and I'm hungry. Would you buy me some food?"

A wave of knowing washed through me. This was the real reason why I was moved to leave the house for food, and I said yes, what do you want?

He looked startled that I'd given him a choice, and then he asked for a three piece meal, and whatever sides came with it. Then he pointed to the walk at the other end of the building. "I'll wait for you there," he said.

I added his order to mine as I got to the window. When I explained who it was for, the cashier thanked me for doing that.

Then the homeless man thanked me and said, God Bless you, when I gave him his food.

I told him I was already blessed to be able to serve, and to enjoy his meal.

I drove home in tears, and then told Scout about his part in helping someone in need tonight.

He nodded. He's quiet like that, but it moved him as much as it did me.

So, the next time the Universe gives you a chance to help, just know what you first set out to do, may reach farther than you could imagine, to help people you will never know.

Sent with peace.

Sent with light.
Sent with love.

&

A long trying day, and yet the only thing I complained about today were the neighbor's dogs, and the only ones who heard me say it were the dogs in this house, so I'm holding my own.

Nothing went as planned, which is proof that plans are meant to be changed.

I have climbed ladders today, and at seventy-six years old, that is not a wise thing to do.

I did not eat food until 3:30 p.m.

I'm not bragging. I'm irked at myself.

That is so not healthy for me to do that, but the day was what it was.

Tomorrow is a whole new day, so it's all good.

Spirit says:

Misplaced trust comes from believing what you hear, and not what you see.

Spirit says:

When you see a truth, and reject it because it does not follow your needs and beliefs, and you choose what you choose because you want to belong, then you have failed yourself.

Once you fail yourself, you take others down with you.

Sent with peace.
Sent with light.
Sent with love.

&

Spirit says:
Opinions are personal.
Being angry because someone does not share yours is actually an immature reaction to not getting your way.

It stems from childhood. The fit you had when you were five.

The pouting when you were seven.

The name calling when you were ten, because something isn't how you want it to go, even though other people are fine with it.

You obviously did not outgrow that behavior.

It is a sign of immaturity.

Maturity has less to do with age, and more to do with the growth of compassion and humanity within you.

With maturity comes understanding.

Understanding that what makes you happy, can be someone else's trigger for a different emotion.

You can ignore other people's rights.

You can turn away from justice, if that is your choice.

You can look at a truth and still not see it, because you have locked yourself into a mindset that does not allow for adjustable parameters.

Once you have decided it is your right to set yourself up as judge and jury to the world, and that everyone who has a different opinion from yours is not only wrong, but plotting against you at every turn, then that is where you are.

And in that place, you will find your tribe of like-minded people, and you will hate, and you will complain together.

And that is your choice.

But your choice is like your opinion.

It's personal.

Expecting others to think like you is still immaturity.

And in this way, nothing can change.

What goes around, comes around - including ignorance of life.

Sent with peace.
    Sent with light.
    Sent with love.

Spirit says:
There will always be more messages.
But I had to stop somewhere, and this was it.

I have released two other books of posts similar to this in previous years.

The first was called *Steering From The Backseat*.

The second was *The Light Within Us*.

My prayer for you as you read this book, is that you receive answers you've been seeking, and maybe a little comfort, too.

Sent with peace.
    Sent with light.
    Sent with love.